SEEDS OF CONTENTION

SEEDS OF CONTENTION

World Hunger and the Global Controversy
over GM Crops

Per Pinstrup-Andersen and Ebbe Schiøler

The Johns Hopkins University Press
Baltimore & London

9 8 7 6 5 4 3 2 1

The Johns Hopkins University Press
2715 North Charles Street
Baltimore, Maryland 21218-4363
www.press.jhu.edu

Library of Congress Cataloging-in-Publication Data
Pinstrup-Andersen, Per.
  Seeds of contention : world hunger and the global controversy
over GM crops / Per Pinstrup-Andersen and Ebbe Schiøler.
    p. cm.
  Includes bibliographical references and index.
  ISBN 0-8018-6826-2
  1. Food supply. 2. Food supply—Developing countries.
3. Crops—Genetic engineering—Economic aspects. 4. Crops—
Genetic engineering—Economic aspects—Developing countries.
5. Agriculture—Economic aspects. I. Schiøler, Ebbe. II. Title.
HD9000.5.P564 2001
338.1'6—dc21   2001002303

A catalog record for this book is available from the British Library.

CONTENTS

FOREWORD

"A person who has food has many problems. A person who has no food has only one problem," says a Chinese proverb. Per Pinstrup-Andersen and Ebbe Schiøler suggest that whether genetically modified food is seen as a boon or a bane depends partly on a person's social location. The authors choose to locate themselves in solidarity with poor people. "The poor should be given the opportunity to decide for themselves" may be the most important sentence in this book, because hunger is not only about lack of food, or even lack of capital, it's also finally about powerlessness— the lack of ability to choose.

No one voluntarily dies of undernutrition and related diseases. People in the industrialized world can choose whether or not to eat genetically modified potato chips or take genetically modified prescription drugs with their morning orange juice. They should not prevent people in the developing world from having the opportunity to make their own choices.

This book raises important questions about the role of various strategies to combat hunger. Who should own new technologies that are based on native grains or public goods. Can we trust profit-driven corporations? Will corporations spend money to develop food products for the parts of the world where people need it most but have the least ability to pay for it?

How much should we trust science? If there's one thing we should know by the beginning of the twenty-first century, it is that science and technology do not provide panaceas. The Green Revolution saved millions of lives, and yet the folks who brought us penicillin and the computer also brought us germ warfare, the ICBM, and ozone depletion.

The public "debate" has not been very constructive. The public discussion has mostly been a war of perceptions. *Seeds of Contention* moves past tainted words and juiced-up reporting by providing a sane and careful analysis of what is known, and not known, about genetically modified foods as a solution to the problem of hunger. The book is an invitation to fair, open, and nuanced public discussion. The long-term effects of genetically modified foods remain uncertain and potentially risky. But then so is the morning commute to work or the flight to visit grandma. The risks of using genetically modified foods have to be carefully weighed against what they could do to reduce hunger and environmental destruction. We who have reaped such huge benefits from gene manipulation in medicine should remain open to new agricultural products that might save thousands of lives.

Pinstrup-Andersen and Schiøler sometimes answer the questions they raise and other times point in the direction where the answers are likely to be found. They say what works in one part of the world will be different than what works somewhere else. There are "no silver bullets." They recommend a progressive conservatism—an approach that would encourage innovations, including biotech, that have the potential to help end hunger, but that would do the testing, check the evidence, and be wary of single-solution proposals. Genetically modified foods are not *the* solution to hunger but are part of a larger solution that relies most heavily on traditional methods in agriculture.

There are two salutary meta-themes in the book—morality and politics. Both proponents and opponents of genetically modified foods use moral arguments. One side claims that genetically modified foods might bring lasting destruction to the environment, human health, and the well-being of poor people; the other argues that GMOs have the potential to alleviate hunger and poverty while improving the quality of the environment. Both sides claim the moral high ground, but the best path is probably somewhere between the extremes.

The other meta-theme is politics. This book is written for a popular audience. The authors assume that public opinion really matters, that an informed and aroused citizenry can affect the outcome of the debate through politics. Hunger is a problem we can solve. But governments must do their part. Bread for the World members and others have successfully lobbied Congress for debt relief to help hungry people in the poorest countries. This victory has led to a revival of hope that world hunger can be cut in half by 2015. The U.S. government could do its part by committing an additional 1 billion dollars a year to poverty-focused foreign assistance to Africa—the place where hunger is deepest and getting worse. That's equivalent to a penny per day per American.

The funding should include support for public research and testing on biotech agriculture. Private firms take public agricultural products and then modify their genes. But then those companies own the outcomes, and they seldom find it profitable to develop and market products for poor people. Someone has to look out for the well-being of poor people. And that someone is mainly government—the protector of the common good, the defender of the public interest, the agency with the resources and capacity to bring about large-scale results.

This book is stuffed like a Thanksgiving turkey with interesting examples that are grounded in sound science. The authors are to be congratulated for explaining difficult issues in such a readable and engaging way, without compromising the scientific integrity for which the International Food Policy Research Institute is so well known. I recommend this book to all who are concerned about ending hunger.

DAVID BECKMANN
President, Bread for the World and
Bread for the World Institute

PREFACE

One cannot follow events in the media for long before coming across stories, comments, or letters to the editor on the use of genetic engineering in food and agriculture. And often, the slant taken is negative. Most of those who voice their opinions or report on the battles surrounding gene technology seem to be opposed to it. In the opposite camp are farmers, researchers, and some private corporations, who are at pains to emphasize the potential of this new technology. Then, somewhere in the middle, is the large share of consumers who are trying to make sense of the debate.

Forming the almost silent majority in this international debate are the people of the developing countries. Amidst all the polemic, their interests and their options are heavily downplayed, except when they are used as pawns. This is regrettable, since an extremely important aspect of the fundamental debate on the use of genetic engineering in food and agriculture is thus overlooked: what good can it do?

We cannot claim, with any justification, that we speak in this book on behalf of the developing countries. On the contrary, we believe that too many well-to-do individuals and groups from Europe and North America have taken an unacceptably paternalistic position, claiming to represent the interests of the developing countries and to know what is best for the poor within these countries. Instead, we propose that the poor should be given the opportunity to decide for themselves.

Our aim is to illustrate the gravity of the food situation for farmers and consumers in developing countries and to point to some realistic ways in which genetic engineering can help improve the situation without taking unacceptable risks, if people in developing countries choose to do so. This technology needs to be handled responsibly, and we have cited a number of essential requirements for the safe application of genetic engineering and its end products in the food sector in developing countries.

Neither of us is a biologist, nor are we particularly enamored of technology. We both have worked for many years on developing-world issues, agricultural research, and food policy. Therefore, this book is not a scientific treatise on modern biotechnology and it makes only limited reference to academic sources. But it is based on a wealth of formal and informal source materials, as well as studies carried out by a host of researchers, including the staff of the International Food Policy Research Institute, whose director general is one of the authors of this book.

This book is a revised and updated version of a book published in Denmark in fall 2000. We are grateful to a number of people for their help in producing this edition. Our thanks go in particular to Barbara J. Haveland for translating the Danish text and to Phyllis Skillman, Linda Strange, and Heidi Fritschel for editorial assistance.

PER PINSTRUP-ANDERSEN

EBBE SCHIØLER

INTRODUCTION

What Is the Debate All About?

Do you recall the reports about the threat to the monarch butterfly, widely publicized in the early summer of 1999? Laboratory research conducted in the United States showed that monarch caterpillars died after eating pollen from a new variety of genetically modified corn (maize). The media outcry on behalf of this much-loved butterfly was long and loud. The culprit clearly was modern science run amok.

Do you recall reading the story, in the same summer, about a village in southwestern Zimbabwe where a skinny three-year-old girl, exhausted from weeks of fever and barely supported by occasional feedings of thin porridge, lay dying on a mat, surrounded by crying relatives? Of course you don't recall this. It was not reported, because the media were not there. And the outcry? This did not extend beyond the confines of the girl's small village.

As it happens, the two stories are intertwined. They are both about food—for the haves and the have-nots—and how we produce it, now and in the future. Unfortunately, only the story of the endangered butterfly was a matter of public discussion. Later in the year, though, the butterfly story was discredited by new research—monarchs in their natural habitat had suffered no harm from the genetically modified crop. This time, most of the media did not bother to carry the story.

Science, building on the work of generations of farmers and of earlier researchers, has produced a new tool with the potential to make agriculture more productive and more environmentally friendly, and even to make crops more nutritious. Agricultural biotechnology, including the use of genetic engineering to create new varieties of food crops, is not without its risks, as critics in the industrialized countries have been quick to point out. But the heated debate in Europe is showing signs of drowning out all serious consideration of the important promise this technology holds for the poor in developing countries—people for whom the risk calculation may involve not a small price difference at the grocery store but the difference between food for their families and hunger, between life and death.

In the industrialized countries, a number of questions usually arise about agricultural biotechnology and genetically modified (GM) food:

- Is GM food safe to eat?
- How will the technology affect the environment?
- What will happen to wild plants, insects, birds?
- Will consumers be offered a reasonable choice based on solid information?
- How will traditional agriculture and rural life be affected?
- Will companies such as Monsanto have too much power?
- Should the patenting of modified genes be permitted?
- Are we using science ethically?
- Are we playing God?

These are important questions, and the answers have great weight for millions of people—millions of mainly well-fed, essentially healthy people. But other questions rarely make it onto the list:

- How can this technology improve the quality of the food we eat?
- Will it boost agricultural productivity?
- Can it be of benefit to the poor populations of developing countries?

These questions are the topic of this book.

Taking a balanced view of the potential and the risks of agricultural biotechnology is neither easy nor popular at the moment, and the debate on the pros and cons seems somewhat like a battleground. From one trench, Mae-Wan Ho, a biologist at the Open University in the United Kingdom, shouts, "Genetic engineering biotechnology is an unprecedented intimate alliance between bad science and big business, which will spell the end of humanity as we know it, and the end of the world at large."[1] And Lord Melchett, director of Greenpeace U.K., also voices his concern: "Genetically modified crops pose a greater threat to the environment than nuclear wastes or chemical pollution."[2] From the opponent's trench comes the response of the chairman of the agricultural conglomerate Monsanto: "After all, we are the technical experts. We know we are right. The 'antis' obviously don't really understand the science and are just as obviously pushing a hidden agenda, probably to destroy capitalism."[3] Thus the adversarial positions harden.

We must look elsewhere for a cooler consideration of this question. In the summer of 1999, Britain's respected Nuffield Council on Bioethics published an analysis of the ethical and social aspects of the application of genetic modification technology to agricultural plants. In its summing up, the report steers a middle course: "We reaffirm our view that GM crops represent an important new technology which ought to have the potential to do much good in the world, provided that proper safeguards are maintained or introduced."[4]

The Monsanto chairman is right about one thing, however. The science involved is not well understood. Simplifications abound and lead easily to an atmosphere of fear-mongering. "Genes are spreading in the wild," reads a headline in a Danish newspaper,[5] implying that this is cause for alarm. Why so? After all, the spread of genes is very old news indeed, underlying the entire evolutionary process in the plant kingdom. Should we not look at genes as the biological information units in any living cell? No, say the fear-mongers, genes are those dangerous little thingamajigs that researchers are shamelessly juggling—in the hope of making a fortune. So it is only natural that consumers and supermarkets, as the media report, crave "gene-free" foods. Meeting such a demand would be as impossible as delivering "chemical-free" food, as claimed on some labels.

Likewise, familiar agricultural products developed with traditional breeding techniques are sometimes labeled "natural" to distinguish them from those developed with biotechnology—this in spite of the well-established, sophisticated methods, the expensive equipment, and the long laboratory hours that often go into traditional breeding. Not much food would be available if nature's original contribution had not been improved upon.

As we show in this book, caution about the use of GM crops is warranted. Fear is not. But the fear is having its effect. For example, an Indian nongovernmental organization opposed the United States' sending food aid that included GM foods to the Indian state of Orissa. The lot was, in the eyes of the organization, "genetically contaminated."[6] And a private organization based in England asked, "Are GM crops the next in line of inappropriate products to be dumped on poor countries?"[7]

Part of the sentiment against GM crops springs from distrust of the multinational companies that have developed many of these products. The multinationals are accused of stopping at nothing in the battle for customers in the rural areas of developing countries, resorting to such ploys as "free seed trials, special open days [in test fields], misleading promotions, golf tournaments and credits."[8] The distrust of private corporations, of course, is not limited to the area of GM food. Unethical behavior by some corporations can cast a shadow on all of them.[9] But even if we accept that some multinationals' practices may have undermined public confidence in their activities, should this block all rational judgment about the usefulness of a technology that could be developed by publicly funded research for the benefit of the hungry families of the developing world?

Indeed, if we take the time to listen, we can hear voices from the developing world in opposition to this outright rejection of agri-cultural biotechnology. Cyrus Ndiritu, director of Kenya's Institute for Agricultural Research, has said, "The on-going debate emerging especially from Europe about the real and perceived hazards of bi-otechnology in Africa can be taken as being aimed at creating fear, mistrust, and general confusion to the public and has failed to seek messages and views of the African policymakers and stakehold-ers."[10] Similarly, Hassan Adamu, the Nigerian minister of agricul-ture, wrote in a *Washington Post* op-ed article in September 2000, "Agricultural biotechnology holds great promise for Africa and other areas of the world where circumstances such as poverty and poor growing conditions make farming difficult . . . To deny des-perate, hungry people the means to control their futures by pre-suming to know what is best for them is not only paternalistic but morally wrong."[11]

This is at the core of the debate. Some see no point in taking ag-ricultural biotechnology further, since we—those of us living in the industrialized world—already have what we need in our supermar-kets. Others regard biotechnology as one more tool to improve the gloomy food prospects of the developing world. Given that the starving three-year-old Zimbabwean girl in our opening story is not an exception but pretty close to the rule in many areas of that country—and in the rest of Africa and large parts of Asia—should we not be open to using every available tool to change the situ-ation, including agricultural biotechnology?

Not necessarily, some argue. Alternative solutions are available. For instance, "The main problem with the food supply is not a question of productivity, but a question of distribution—right?"[12] From the Kenyan point of view, the situation does not seem quite that simple. According to Cyrus Ndiritu, "The notion that, at a global level, the problem is not one of inadequate food production, but of distribution, is correct in a statistical sense, but it is trivial and highly misleading. It suggests, for example, that redistribution of static food production is the solution to food deficiency, and fur-ther, it relegates the need to increase production in regions like Africa to a subsidiary role."[13] Let's assume, though, that the rich world did find the will to set up a massive redistribution program; this would require a huge expenditure—on establishing transportation networks, among other things; would necessarily mean diverting funds from long-term local development and support programs; and fails to take into account that agriculture is the primary occupation in much of the developing world. As we discuss in Chapter 4, there are many excellent reasons why food should be grown where it is consumed.

So in response to the question "do we really need GM foods?" the well-fed consumer might well answer no, not really. But if biotechnology research were directed to solving the problems of poor farmers in developing countries, allowing them to produce crops that yield more, are more nutritious, and can cope with diseases, insect attacks, drought, and infertile soils, the answer to the broader question "does the world need GM foods?" may well be a firm yes! After all, those of us living in the industrialized world would say yes to the use of genetic engineering to develop medicines to solve any human health problem.

The potential for using agricultural biotechnology to fight these problems of the developing world will be lost if the present resistance to genetic modification continues, and even grows, because investors will direct their funds into other areas, and public authorities will regard GM organisms as far too controversial for support. The developing countries cannot go it alone. Here, as in other scientific fields, new discoveries and breakthrough results are shaped in a global dialogue among enthusiastic researchers worldwide.

We discuss all the issues introduced here throughout the book. For now, we leave the last word to a researcher who has been working for many years to develop a better tuberous crop—cassava—for Africa. He reminds us that, ethically, opting out of taking risks may not be the right thing to do, "for there is also a risk involved in always just saying no!"[14] We hope this book helps persuade more people to reconsider that all too easy and undemanding "no!"

1 • AGRICULTURAL RESEARCH

Making a Difference in People's Lives

One of history's most famous prophets of doom was the English clergyman Thomas Malthus. In the late eighteenth century Malthus made the astute observation that population growth would, at some point in a not too distant future, lead to widespread famine, given that farmers would not be able to produce enough food to feed everyone. Mass starvation would then bring about a horrifying—but necessary—reduction in the population, establishing a new balance between the number of people and the food available. Such cycles would recur at regular intervals.

This was a logical conclusion for a scholar of his day. As far back as anyone could remember, the yield per acre of farmland had remained more or less constant, and in Malthus's part of the world not much virgin land was left to put under the plow. Nor was it feasible to transport food products over long distances. So Malthus's gloomy logic seemed perfectly reasonable and carried a lot of weight in his own day and, indeed, into our own time.

While the world's population growth might have been moderate in Malthus's day, it was great enough that its inclusion as a dynamic factor in future projections seemed reasonable. And though farmers' grain yields did increase, they grew slowly, at a rate of less than 0.1 percent per year. Food production was therefore deemed to be a static factor, and a collision between rapid population growth and slow agricultural growth was considered inevitable.

Had Malthus looked farther back as well as forward he might not have been so pessimistic. The average wheat yield in Great Britain rose from between 500 and 700 kilograms per hectare during the Middle Ages to 1.68 tons per hectare in 1850.[1] The situation had improved a good deal by Malthus's time, compared with his father's and his grandfathers' days. But not until the early twentieth century did anything happen to allay the pessimism. Crop yields began to climb steadily and then to soar. Agriculture had become a part of modern society, with science and technology playing a key role.

The Research Factor: Altering the Status Quo

In fact, quite a lot had already been achieved in agriculture by the time the academics and engineers got in on the act. Farmers everywhere, down through the ages, noted which crops gave the best yields. They altered their working methods, fought weeds, spread manure from their livestock on the fields, regularly left sections of the land fallow, and rotated their crops to avoid depleting the soil of its nutrients. And, just as important, they carefully set aside seeds from the sturdiest plants to sow the following year. In every field, weak, robust, and average plants naturally spring up, and it would take a bad farmer—or a disastrously poor harvest—for the second-raters to be set aside for seed. The same principles applied in animal husbandry: the best animals were crossbred, a practice that led in the course of time not only to sturdier, more productive individual breeds but also to entirely new strains. The tireless efforts of generation after generation of farmers paid off in strains of plants and animals now known as *land races*. While such strains have all but vanished from the land in the industrialized world, they are still vital to the existence of many farmers in the developing countries.

Extensive research led to levels of agricultural productivity vastly different from the almost static pattern that had been the norm for centuries the world over. Better education of farmers, generally and in specific areas relevant to farming, was essential for the implementation and consolidation of the newly acquired expertise. Improved soil cultivation, weed control, ways to combat pests and diseases, and the use of fertilizers and irrigation, where necessary, promoted best possible development of plants. The other vital factor was the propagation of more productive plants. This was accomplished by laboratories and seed growers who discovered the work of the Austrian monk Gregor Mendel, which was published in 1866 but had remained more or less unnoticed for decades. Working from Mendel's theories (his laws of heredity) and his carefully detailed experiments, they arrived at new varieties through systematic crossbreeding, selecting offspring that combined the best properties of the parents.

Advances in agriculture during the past century have mirrored those in the health sector. Better living conditions, hygiene, and nursing care brought about major improvements in health and life expectancy, and these advances were further enhanced by the discovery of new medicines and the development of modern medical technology. The hefty boost to the population that resulted led, in turn, to a greater need for more food and hence more productive farming.

Since the beginning of the twentieth century, the balance between improved farming methods and more robust crop and livestock strains has continued to follow the same upward curve. Initially, the new crop varieties did not make a great difference, but yields *did* increase, mainly because growing conditions were so much improved. In England, the average wheat crop increased by approximately 28 percent between 1901 (at which time it was no greater than fifty years earlier) and 1913. But the most dramatic change took place in the next eighty years, when yields more than tripled, rising to almost 7 tons per hectare by 1990. In Ireland the increase was even more impressive, reaching 8.2 tons per hectare by 1990.[2]

This pattern was repeated for many other crops in many countries, not only in the developed regions of the world but also in Asia and Latin America. After centuries of only slight increases, yields suddenly shot up exponentially. The explanation was the same everywhere. First, farmers became more skilled at tending their land as a result of systematic findings about optimum farming conditions; here we see the first upturn in the curve. Then the new crop varieties began to make their presence felt, sparking off an upsurge that in many places is still going strong.

Bleak Outlook for the Developing World

During the years since Malthus first propounded his views, his followers—the neo-Malthusians—have had good reason to insist that their predictions were bound to come true. From time to time certain parts of the world were hit by famine in the wake of crop failure or blight. A famous and heartbreaking example was the massive potato blight in Ireland in the mid-nineteenth century, when widespread famine depopulated whole sections of the country, leading to mass emigration—perhaps escape is a better word—primarily to the United States.

In the densely populated developing countries, in the weeks before harvest, the lives of many hung by a thread. Until quite recently, China and the Indian subcontinent experienced appalling famines if crops failed, and the scale of these disasters was often not apparent until long after the victims were dead and buried. And apart from—and alongside—these crises, in many parts of the world large numbers of people were permanently malnourished.

It was in the populous nations of Asia, in the years following the Second World War, that Malthus's vision seemed likely to come true. The population was increasing fast, while agriculture was still conducted along traditional, not very productive lines. Meanwhile, the growth of agriculture in the developed world showed that a dynamic rise in population could be matched by a dynamic increase in agricultural output—in principle, at least.

Because farming methods and scientific breakthroughs do, in fact, resemble one another only "in principle" from one place to another, findings have to be modified to meet the conditions and demands of different areas. To reduce the threat of famine in Asia, traditional crops from the industrialized countries—wheat, in particular—had to be adapted for this different environment, but better methods of cultivating local crops, primarily rice, also had to be discovered. Both the soil and the climate were different from those in the developed countries, and the chance that research and extension workers would be communicating their discoveries to a well-educated farming community was slim.

And there was no time to lose. In the early 1960s, the wheat yield in India and China was on a par with that of Europe during the Middle Ages—600 to 800 kilograms per hectare. Although the yield for rice was higher, the pattern was also much the same as that seen in European farming in the old days, with little or no rise in annual yields. But in these Asian countries, the gradual introduction of better living conditions and modern health-care techniques led to a drop in the mortality rate, while the birth rate remained steady and the survival rate among young children increased. Both of these heavily populated nations—China and India—and a number of others in that part of the world—the Philippines and Indonesia, for example—relied upon age-old farming traditions that worked well enough as long as the population stayed within reasonable bounds. And down through the ages, people could appropriate new land for farming by clearing forests, establishing fields on hillsides, or cultivating new, drier areas where the farming conditions were not as good. But the expansion of agricultural production through the appropriation of new land was rapidly reaching its limit and the negative environmental effects were becoming more obvious.

Throughout the 1960s, starvation on a truly massive scale was staved off by what the countries themselves could produce, supplemented by foreign aid. This was a short-term measure designed to tide these countries over while scientists in laboratories and test fields at research centers in the Philippines, Mexico, and elsewhere worked flat out to reverse the regions' downward spiral in agriculture.

Turning the Tide: A New Agricultural Package

In the 1950s, two leading American philanthropic institutions, the Ford and Rockefeller foundations, spearheaded the development of techniques and crops capable of producing the sort of results that agriculture in the industrialized countries had achieved only over several generations. Thanks to an initial injection of capital from the two foundations and the efforts of a host of enthusiastic researchers, including many from developing-country institutions, new, high-yielding varieties of wheat and rice were developed, crucially different from the traditional strains in that the plants were shorter and sturdier with a better balance between straw and grain weight. And these plants responded better to fertilizers—a crucial factor, inasmuch as the new, high-yielding varieties were part of a package aimed at revitalizing Asian agriculture. At its best the package included not only new seed but also chemical fertilizers, insecticides to combat plant diseases, and irrigation. Individually, each of these factors could bring about some increase in productivity, but combined they really made a huge difference.

The results of these new agricultural packages were soon visible. Farmers and their families ate better, sent more children to school, and built better houses. As the new crop varieties became more widely used, the average yield rose steadily, just as it had done in the industrialized countries. Since 1961, China has seen an average annual increase in wheat yield per hectare of 91 kilograms. Between 1968 and 1990, India's rice production rose by 50 kilograms per hectare each year.

The initiative taken by the Ford and Rockefeller foundations stimulated other efforts to ensure food security in developing countries. Permanent research stations were established for rice in the Philippines in 1961 (the International Rice Research Institute), and for maize and wheat in Mexico in 1966 (Centro Internacional de Mejoramiento de Maiz y Trigo, CIMMYT).[3] Official development organizations in the industrialized countries decided to pool their resources to help the developing countries, and in 1971 they formed an association called the Consultative Group on International Agricultural Research (CGIAR). The CGIAR has expanded to include sixteen institutions conducting research on all the key crops of the developing world, on livestock production and disease control, fish and aquaculture, forestry and agroforestry, plant genetics, and food policy. One center has been established with the primary purpose of helping developing countries conduct their own research. All research findings are freely available to researchers and all other interested parties worldwide.

During the 1970s, as the threat of famine in Asia dwindled, solid and convincing research findings also brought hope for Latin America and to some extent northern Africa. The CGIAR could not, of course, take all the credit. The new discoveries and techniques and their adaptation to local conditions were achieved in collaboration with national research institutions, while private enterprise and some private research institutions played an important part in ensuring delivery of the necessary ingredients to the villages.

One Picture, Many Interpretations

The transformation in agricultural productivity in many parts of the developing world became known as the Green Revolution. There is something almost mythical about this term, and many—more or less justified—counter-myths have been attached to it.

Before looking at what was achieved, let's recap the initiative's prime motivation: millions of lives were at risk from starvation; results were needed, and fast. This is not to say that measures were taken uncritically, regardless of the cost. But there was never any doubt that an increase in productivity had to be the top priority. We must also emphasize at the outset that the Green Revolution was not a one-off exercise of the 1960s and 1970s. It is an ongoing phenomenon, with results still forthcoming and adjustments constantly being made in the light of new experience.

Criticism of the Green Revolution centers on what it brought in its wake and on what it did not achieve. Let's consider the latter first. Here, as in other contexts, Africa is seen as the forgotten continent, left behind by the Green Revolution. In Africa, critics say, the new varieties and new technologies proved useless or were never given a proper chance. This may be so, but we need to look more closely at what happened in the case of Africa.

In the 1960s the focus of the Green Revolution was on Asia and Latin America; at that time these were the continents most at risk, containing, as they did, the lion's share of the developing world's poor inhabitants. Sub-Saharan Africa supported forms of agriculture and crops that could derive no direct benefit from the technological packages developed for the farming methods practiced in other parts of the developing world. But work was soon under way to develop crops and techniques specifically suited to African agriculture. Today four CGIAR centers have their headquarters in Africa and all have research stations in the region. As a result, crops such as maize, bananas, cassava, and rice have undergone a marked increase in productivity in a number of African countries. Crops neglected by private research because they are of no interest in the industrialized world, such as the root crop cassava and the grain millet, are continually being improved. But soaring population figures take their toll on all these advances; Africa's food production per capita has been falling for many years now. A real revolution in African agriculture is still needed. In sub-Saharan Africa today, crops typically provide a yield at the same level as that in Asia before the Green Revolution—or that in Europe during the Middle Ages.

One example of a research venture geared specifically to Africa is the successful battle, waged through advanced international research, against the pests that attack the cassava plant (see Box 1).

And what of the adverse events that the Green Revolution brought in its wake? One accusation is that it made the rich richer and the poor poorer. This view is not based on any long-term observation of the facts. Critics frequently cite the villages of India as a striking example, pointing out that, as a rule, the large-scale farmers were quicker to exploit the potential of the new technol-

BOX 1

INSECT WARS IN AFRICA'S CASSAVA FIELDS

Imported Insects

In the 1960s an old acquaintance—the cassava mealy bug—made its presence felt in the West African countryside. It had been introduced, as the biologists put it, by accident, from South America. It ate and ate, spreading rapidly eastward, and the situation looked totally disastrous for the cassava. The researchers were at their wits' end. Cassava is a major crop in South America, but oddly enough the cassava mealy bug has posed no problem there, and so little research has gone into it.

As if this were not enough, in 1971 another nasty pest, the cassava green spider mite, showed up, also from South America. It was first discovered in Uganda, where it seemed to feel very much at home, and spread from there.

Both of these insects can ruin anywhere from 30 to 50 percent of a harvest. But one needs to know that it is, in fact, insects that are doing the damage, because it takes an extraordinarily powerful microscope and a trained eye to spot them.

A Natural Reaction

It took many years and a lot of experiments to reach a solution to the problem. There had to be a good explanation for why the cassava mealy bug, which the researchers turned their attention to first, was not a problem in South America.

Two international research centers: CIAT (Centro Internacional de Agricultura Tropical) in Colombia and IITA (International Institute of Tropical Agriculture) in Nigeria, instituted a search for the mealy bug in Brazil, a country that grows a lot of cassava. After much research, they discovered that the bug was held in check by parasitic wasps, although none of those species that were tested in the net cages of the laboratories really rose to the bait.

Fresh expeditions to diverse corners of South America eventually unearthed several promising parasitic wasps. The trick was to find out which of these was the most effective. Numerous requirements had to be met: it could not be harmful to useful insects or carry any disease into Africa; it had to be able to survive conditions in the African cassava belt, which can vary greatly over such a wide area; and it had to have an insatiable appetite and still be able to survive when mealy bugs were not so plentiful.

One small wasp appeared to be a likely candidate. It was transferred from South America to a laboratory in London where it could be certified as disease-free and be hatched by the thousands. Tests in the fields in West Africa lived up to all expectations, and the wasp cut a swath along the trail left by the mealy bug. It was usually deposited in small batches in the stricken areas, but occasionally dropped from airplanes.

Easier and Easier

A team of highly specialized researchers had been assigned to the project and the most modern methods and instruments were employed in order to obtain the desired objective. After that it was a case of developing a technique that could be replicated even in the most modest laboratories in Africa. And it was the IITA scientists who came up with the simple and ingenious solution to producing the wasps, locally, by the millions.

The Ugandan researchers at the research station in Namulonge are now running the system themselves. The entire production set-up consists of no more than a sleeve of thin plastic, 1.5 meters in length, filled with sawdust and suspended from a cord. Above this hangs a small bucket with a hose for watering the sawdust. Lots of little holes have been cut in the plastic bag. Short lengths of cassava stalk are stuck into the holes and before long these put out roots and leaves, giving the impression of a little Christmas tree of cassava cuttings. The cassava plant really can get by with very little nourishment.

The tree is transferred into a tent made of very fine mosquito netting, into which the destructive mealy bugs are then released. They come from little net cages in which they have gorged themselves on cassava leaves. Their delight in all this fresh guzzling potential is short-lived, however, as cassava branches crawling with parasitic wasps are inserted into the tent. Now it is the wasps' turn to feed, and this they do in record time.

This process can quietly go on until such time as the wasps are needed somewhere else. When that happens, the lower part of the tent is covered with a length of black fabric and the wasps crawl up toward the light at the top and into a little canister of clear plastic.

Within 12 hours, most of the wasps are inside the plastic canister, which is then packed into a cool box (complete with cooling elements), to keep the wasps subdued. Thereafter, it is a matter of getting out to the field before the temperature rises. The wasps are released onto the stricken field and soon have things under control.

The very first such operation took place in Uganda, when the mealy bug turned up there in 1992. In those days the Ugandans were not equipped to tackle the problem themselves, but within 12 hours of the discovery, IITA had flown in a consignment of parasitic wasps. After that it was only a three-hour drive in the little cool box before the battle for "biological control" commenced.

Green Is Not Always Good

Having learned from their experiences with the mealy bug, the researchers could—in theory, at any rate—calculate that the other pest, the cassava green spider mite, would also be susceptible to biological control. Attempts had been made to spray it with insecticide, but for many good reasons—primarily financial ones—these never really came to anything.

The international research centers therefore dispatched new expeditions to various parts of South America, and five different predator mites captured in Colombia were tried out against the cassava green spider mite. Between 1984 and 1988, 5.2 million predator mites were deployed at 341 locations in 11 African countries. None survived, presumably because they could find no other food once they had eaten the cassava mites.

It was an expensive lesson, and the next attempt focused specifically on locating predator mites from regions with climates more closely resembling those in Africa. There was a lot riding on the second deployment, too. Five different predator mites were dropped off at 365 points, again in 11 countries, between 1989 and 1995. Three of these did fairly well.

The big surprise proved to be a predator mite not included in the experiment until 1993. It can now be found in over 1,000 districts in both East and West Africa: a lively character, capable, in its first season, of ranging 12 kilometers from the drop-off point and, in the second year, of traveling up to 200 kilometers. It now covers over 400,000 square kilometers. This predator mite, which has both a first and a last name—*Typhlodromalus aripo*—also lives on pollen, the nectar from flowers, and the sap of plants, so even when the number of cassava mites is falling off, it manages to survive. It can produce two generations for every one of the green mite's, so it is not much of a contest.

In fact this predator mite has more than paid its way. Researchers have calculated that when the predator mite is let loose in a field attacked by the cassava green spider mite, production rises by between 30 and 40 percent. In West Africa alone this has resulted in a gain of US$48.5 million per year.

Source: Ebbe Schiøler, "Without Poison, But Naturally," in *Good News from Africa* (Washington, D.C.: International Food Policy Research Institute, 1998).

ogy than were the smaller farmers. This outcome was unavoidable. Even though small-scale farmers would like to produce more and earn more, their first concern must be to avoid loss, so they seldom dare to risk everything on a new technique or variety. But once they see the results achieved on the larger farms, they become as actively involved as large-scale farmers. And where water, fertilizer, and insecticides are readily available, they are used on farms of all sizes.

The International Food Policy Research Institute (IFPRI), a CGIAR center, has carried out one of the few long-term surveys of the effects of the Green Revolution at the village level, conducted in the district of North Arcot, in the not too prosperous southernmost part of India.[4] The study, which compared the 1983–84 and 1973–74 crop seasons, revealed that the small farmers of the district kept abreast of new farming techniques and new varieties of grain. Contrary to the critics' predictions, the growth in agricultural production did not result in a concentration of land in the hands of fewer people. Average incomes rose dramatically over the decade, almost doubling for farmers growing rice on irrigated land (compared with a 40 percent increase for those farming nonirrigated land). Farm laborers also noticed a marked improvement in income. The extra income was spent mainly on food: measured in both calories and protein, the family larder was much better stocked than before. The economic life of the area received a tremendous shot in the arm, thanks to the higher incomes from farming and the resulting demand for both goods and services. In rural areas, the incomes of the poorer inhabitants underwent a greater percentage increase than did those of their more prosperous neighbors, while in the towns the reverse was true, with private enterprises run by the well-to-do reaping the greatest benefit from increased consumer demand.

But How Green Was This Revolution?

Another criticism of the Green Revolution is the adverse effect on the environment of the wholesale use of agrochemicals and vast irrigation systems. There is no doubt that such criticism is justified. In certain parts of Asia severe damage has been done where evaporation of irrigation water over many years has saturated large areas of land with salt. And it cannot be denied that human beings and animals have been damaged by crop spraying.

When the Green Revolution was initiated, even in the more technologically advanced societies, an extremely cavalier attitude was taken toward the risks inherent in the new technology. Low-flying aircraft spraying insecticide over turnip fields were simply considered a sign of progress, whether in Denmark or the state of Wisconsin. This attitude held during the relatively long spell from the end of the Second World War to the 1970s, following the publication of Rachel Carson's seminal work *Silent Spring* in 1962. Nitrate pollution caused by excessive and inappropriate use of fertilizers in industrialized agriculture cannot be excused by saying we did not know any better. And it is not as though, at any time in the last hundred years, American and European farmers have needed to produce increasing quantities of food simply to support survival.

Another factor that must be taken into account is that the extra food needed by the developing countries had to be provided either by an increase in productivity on farmed land or through the appropriation of virgin and, in many cases, fragile land for agriculture. While the cultivation of new tracts of land was a viable solution in some countries, in many others any more drastic inroads into as yet uncultivated land could be undertaken only to the detriment of the surrounding countryside, entailing a loss of vital natural resources. CIMMYT, the center conducting research into maize and wheat, has calculated that, without the scientific breakthroughs associated with the Green Revolution, the increase in India's wheat production alone between 1966 and 1993 would have necessitated plowing up another 40 million hectares of land.[5] If no yield increase had taken place in developing countries since the 1960s, an additional 300–500 million hectares would have been needed.[6] Or, to put it another way, were it not for the achievements of agricultural researchers, much land poorly suited for agriculture would have been plowed up at a high cost to the environment.[7] Wildlife would have suffered, biodiversity would have been reduced, more forests would have been cut down, and land degradation would have been rampant.

Here we need to return to the idea of the Green Revolution as an ongoing process. Work is still under way as researchers strive to develop agricultural techniques and seed varieties that meet both production needs and environmental goals. The Rockefeller Foundation's British president, Gordon Conway, has dubbed this endeavor "the Doubly Green Revolution."[8] The first of the new crop varieties were less likely to bend in the middle and flop to the ground close to harvest time. They were also heavily reliant on all the ingredients in the support package—water, fertilizer, pesticides—and, in a number of areas, were less well equipped to cope with the prevailing local conditions than were the land races they replaced. The one clear point in their favor was their higher yield.

Fresh Aspects of Research Findings

New properties are continually being bred into agricultural plants, and all the latest crops have a certain amount of immunity to common plant diseases and some resistance to pests, while retaining their high-yield advantage. New varieties make more efficient use of the nutrients in the soil, and many can survive on less water than their predecessors. This kind of crop meets the needs of small-scale farmers—in Africa, for example—who cannot afford to use commercial fertilizers and insecticides and who aim to keep the risks of losing a crop low.

To cite one example, in southern Africa, CIMMYT has made great strides in the development of a maize that can withstand drought. A comparative study showed that under optimum growing conditions, the best CIMMYT varieties gave the second-best yield (4 to 7 percent less than the top scorer) of all the maize varieties tested, the majority of which were propagated by local seed manufacturers for use by commercial farmers. But the crucial difference for a farmer faced with an uncertain rainfall is that, when the rains failed, the CIMMYT maize came out the clear winner, with a 40 to 50 percent better yield than varieties that had the highest yields under optimum conditions. This is not far from the win-win situation that small-scale farmers crave and CIMMYT is working toward.[9]

Even so, the "doubly green" is possibly too limited a revolution, given that there is much more to modern agricultural research than just a profitable growth in yield and responsible management of natural resources. Social factors such as poverty, dietary considerations, and gender equality also must be taken into account when establishing priorities for the development of new crops. In this book we look primarily at how to increase productivity and reduce risks in an environmentally sound fashion, but we also discuss other aspects of responsible current research work.

Box 2 presents a brief summary of a recent, broad-based research project involving a number of the aspects outlined above. This research is being carried out at one of the CGIAR centers, the West Africa Rice Development Association, which has its headquarters in the Côte d'Ivoire and conducts research into the development of rice-based cropping systems in Africa.

BOX 2
GETTING THE RICE RIGHT

Rice has been grown in Africa for at least 3,500 years—not the varieties of rice that are grown in the low-lying plains of Asia, where fields are flooded and the rice slops about in water for most of its growing season. The indigenous African rice gets by on rainwater and is sown in the same, familiar manner as other grains. It does well here on Cote d'Ivoire. It can take most of what the climate has to offer and is resistant to numerous diseases and harmful insects. But its yield is not what one might call impressive, and so most farmers concentrate on growing one of the imported Asian varieties that do not grow in flooded fields. In a good year the harvest is considerably better with the Asian rice. But not every year is a good year. Far from it: the rains may fail, or an outbreak of some serious plant disease may occur, or insects may attack. In such years one would do better to stick to the African rice. A wise farmer grows a little of both.

Damned Weed

But then there are the weeds. In the fields around here, the weeds we are talking about are not benign little plants like dandelions or buttercups or ground elder. They are stout thistles, coarse grasses, large thick-leaved plants with tough stalks, and little bushes that in next to no time can produce a powerful, deep-reaching root system that chokes everything in sight, if regular, thorough weeding is not carried out.

And weeding in itself poses a major problem, with farm labor so scarce. Everything is done by hand and hoe, and even though the children do their bit, it is still touch and go. It takes 40 days of sweating and straining each year to keep just 1 hectare of land weed-free. And that is one good reason why the African rice is still popular: it is a speedy grower and in no time at all can spread into a whole little bush of densely packed leaves, which cover the soil and overshadow the weeds, making it hard for them to grow.

But, as mentioned previously, this rice does not yield a great crop, no matter how carefully it is tended, not even when given plenty of manure. This particular strain of rice does not produce very many grains per plant, and if its growing conditions are improved, it simply puts out stronger shoots and leaves.

A good many bad things can be said of the African rice. It has the unfortunate knack of shattering, so that some of the barely ripened grains of rice fall onto the ground and are lost before they can be harvested. And the stem is so thin that it will often snap or be bent by the wind and rain. And some of the rice, down in the shade between the leaves, may not ripen. The seed also takes a long time to germinate after sowing. But the grains are fine and the rice tastes good.

At WARDA, the West African Rice Development Association, they have been working for some years on the improvement of African rice. But there is a definite limit to how much can be achieved, and so there has been no great interest in pursuing that particular avenue.

But then again, a lot of work has been invested in adapting and improving the Asian rice varieties. The idea has, in fact, been to reproduce the excellent results achieved in Asia, where record harvests have been produced, year after year, from the 1960s right up until recently. The same formula was applied at WARDA: new varieties and plenty of fertilizer, water, and insecticides where necessary to combat disease and insects. Only about 20 percent of the farmers in West Africa have been able to follow this method.

Over the years the Asian rice has also been rendered more resistant to disease and insects, though it is still not as hardy as its African counterparts. And the Asian varieties did not help at all with the weed problem. On the contrary, they grow tall, slender, and well spread out, allowing their rivals plenty of scope. Consequently, the fields had to be sprayed with weed killer if there was to be any hope of attaining the splendid returns that can be gained from the Asian rice.

This was never an option for smallholders, and so they had to make do with poorer returns and a little of each of the two types of rice in their fields. But there was never a question of whether to grow rice, because in many countries in West Africa, rice is the staff of life. But these countries are by no means capable of producing all that is needed themselves. For every 10 kilos eaten in Cote d'Ivoire, 4 are imported. And the pattern is more or less the same for the rest of West Africa, which, as a whole, imports more than 6 million tons of rice per year. It is hard to picture such a mountain of rice.

Clearly, then, the rice researchers have more than enough to do.

A good rice plant must be able to flourish without the aid of fertilizer; it must be capable of coping with a dry year; and of course it has to provide a decent yield. The rice grains should be large, the panicles firm, and the plants tall: harvesting can be backbreaking work. Besides, tall rice plants are generally believed to produce a good crop. But it is also important that the rice should grow fast and ripen early, so that the gap between using up and replenishing rice stocks will not be so long. And what about weed control? Well, it almost goes without saying that this is most important, if one knows anything about farming.

An Almost Hopeless Task

When a new generation of international researchers joined WARDA in the early 1990s, they went right back to the beginning. Not that the improvements already made on the African and Asian varieties of rice were less than successful, but they never led to any real breakthrough. So the new researchers set themselves the goal of cross-breeding the Asian and the African strains, in an attempt to get the best out of both types. One might think that that would be easy if one knew nothing about crossing plants. In fact, it was a major undertaking, and there were many times when things looked far from hopeful before a successful outcome was reached.

The researchers began by collecting seeds from all of the varieties of African rice they could lay their hands on, from other research centers throughout the world and from WARDA's own seed collection. This gave them a grand total of 1,500 varieties. Since there were many of these about which little was known, they were grown in trial plots and descriptions of each entered in a large catalog. One long page was devoted to each rice plant, giving 47 facts concerning height, thickness of the stem, how many leaves it was capable of producing, how quickly the seed germinated, the length of the panicle, the number of grains, the size of the grains, their color and shape, and of course how it tasted. This catalog also included a great deal of other information, chiefly regarding how well the plants grew and how well they thrived with and without fertilizer and with limited amounts of rain.

Much was already known about the Asian rice. Not least by WARDA's colleagues at the International Rice Research Institute (IRRI) in the Philippines, where they have well over 100,000 seed varieties at their fingertips.

A selection was thus made from among the most promising plants possessing several good qualities from each of the two types that seemed likely to thrive in West Africa. These then had to be crossed this way and that, to bring out the very best in the new plants. There really should be many different plants to choose from, since their performance can vary greatly from place to place in a region as vast as West Africa, with so many different types of soil, different patterns of disease, different insects, and wide variations in the amount of rainfall. Now the hard work really began.

If the pollen of female and male rice plants is mingled, this will, as a rule, result in plants bearing grains of rice. But, as the researchers discovered, these cannot germinate. And that, one might think, would be the end of that. Not, however, at WARDA, because the researchers there knew that in nature, such cross-pollinations do occur now and then. Hence, over the course of the thousands of years in which wild and cultivated species of rice have been in existence, a major process of regeneration occasionally occurs. Researchers can cite instances of this also having been achieved in the laboratories.

So it was simply a matter of perseverance. And sure enough, a tiny percentage of hybrids was induced to germinate in the next generation. The offspring were a little on the spindly side and most of the plants were the exact image of one or the other of their parents, but a handful in each test turned out to be a mixture of both. All efforts now had to be concentrated on these, but there is no denying that it was a slow process: the new plants had to be tended through several generations to make them hardy enough to survive in the outside world. And a rice plant takes at least 120 days to ripen.

More Good Ideas

The researchers therefore cast about for ways of speeding up the process. Other researchers in China and Colombia taught them techniques that enabled them to make direct crosses between the seedlings after only a few weeks. Granted, this meant that they had to develop certain substances in which the plants could grow, but this too they succeeded in doing. Within just two years, they had a small selection of plants ready for use, something which, with the old methods, would have taken at least five or six years.

While all this was going on, work was also being done to improve the parent plants, and the selection process itself was made more exacting. Then the fun really began. All right, so that might not be exactly the word that the researchers would use, but one can tell simply by looking at them that that is what they are thinking.

In the spring of 1996 they rented fields from farmers in a number of villages, and employed people from the villages to work them. Sixty different varieties were planted: two small plots for each variety, one with and one without fertilizer. African and Asian varieties were used, plus 10 of the new hybrids.

Plenty New under the Sun

The researchers have made a radical break with tradition. Previously, they would have spent years working in the test fields back at the research center before finally selecting a couple of new varieties, "the cream of the crop," which could then be offered to the farmers. In this case, all the options are presented and the farmers themselves make the selection. In Ponoundogou in 1997, they grew a total of 19 varieties. Some were rejected as the tests progressed, since the taste, the cooking time, the color of the grains, and the ease with which they can be ground down into flour also had to be assessed under actual conditions.

No surveys have yet been made of the yields obtained by the farmers: the tiny plot of land that can be sown from a packet of rice seed is not enough on which to base any scientific statistics. But on WARDA's test fields it is easy to see what can be achieved, with and without fertilizer; and the new hybrids consistently yield considerably more than their parents, even when no fertilizer is used. If fertilizer is applied, the new varieties can easily match the best of the Asian strains.

But the new varieties also have all the good points that each of their parents boasted: tall sturdy stems, dense foliage at the foot of the plant, speedy growth, no shattering of unripe seeds, and resistance to many common diseases and insects. The new plants also cope well with dry spells. And believe it or not, they have their own built-in scarecrow: the spiky leaves at the very top form a circlet that sticks up into the air, making it hard for the birds to get anywhere near the grains. It is doubtful whether the researchers considered this side-effect when they selected the plants. Nonetheless, they are justifiably proud, even of this last little touch.

Source: Ebbe Schiøler, "Getting the Rice Right," in *Good News from Africa* (Washington, D.C.: International Food Policy Research Institute, 1998).

Raising the Ceiling

In their efforts to increase agricultural productivity, researchers examine results at three levels. First, they look at the actual yield on a working farm in a specific area—the de facto production level. Second, they compare this figure with the yield obtained under controlled growing conditions at local research stations—the current maximum possible yield. Third, they project what the yield could be after further research and development. To this simple triad, they add any properties other than yield that they are seeking. For the sake of simplicity, here we concentrate on yield.

Researchers face several problems in working on these three levels. First, maintaining a steady yield in the field takes some doing, given that plants must withstand a constant succession of attacks from different pests. The insect population varies and, insofar as plants can fend for themselves, they require a continuous updating of their defense mechanisms. Researchers must combat new forms of attack by enabling plants to develop resistance to pests and diseases through mutation. This is routine maintenance research work. For every crop variety currently in use in farmers' fields, researchers and seed growers must have one or more alternatives on hand, ready to be propagated into seed at short notice.

The second major task is limiting the number of factors that prevent the working farmer from obtaining yields as high as those achieved by the research stations in their test fields; researchers talk of "closing the yield gap." Of course, farmers could not make a profit if they invested as heavily in their fields as do researchers in their test plots. From a practical point of view, the economically acceptable level is quite a bit below the yield ceiling. But improvements in certain farming techniques, such as treatment of the soil, weed control, sowing times, and fertilizing schedules, are almost always feasible. This side of agricultural research calls for close collaboration between researchers and farmers. In high-yielding, industrialized agriculture, the main function of research at this level might actually be to map out where farm work can be reduced with the least possible drop in yield, in order to ease the strain on the environment and labor requirements.

The most advanced research work—at the third level—is directed toward raising the actual yield ceiling. When all the possibilities for improving yields through better cultivation have been exhausted, then new plant varieties have to be developed: researchers must undertake a major long-term research project involving the crossing of existing commercial varieties, land races, and wild relatives of cultivated plants. To this end, researchers and seed growers have access, within their own institutions or those of their national and international colleagues, to large seed collections, so-called *gene banks* (see Box 3).

In the industrialized countries of the world, the gap between the results—yield potential and other properties of the crops—on farms and on research stations is not that great, so it does not necessarily follow that the yield gap should be narrowed; yields are normally more or less confined to a set proportion of a crop's maximum yield. In most developing countries, however, the shortfall is still considerable. The gap can, in some cases, be closed by keeping farmers better informed, but often they have neither the workforce nor the money to alter the way they farm and so they do not get the maximum yield from good plant material. This is by no means an unusual situation in many parts of Africa where, for example, the soil is disastrously low in nutrients but farmers cannot afford to add even the tiny amounts of fertilizer that could make all the difference.

BOX 3
GENE BANKS

Over the past hundred years, seeds collected from every corner of the world have been cultivated under stringent test conditions and their various properties recorded. Scientists have then stored samples of the cultivated seeds in the deep freezes of gene banks for future use.

Gene banks, private and public, are to be found in almost every country, and the task of expanding and maintaining the collections is an enormous one. These seed stores must be continually regenerated through cultivation, since the seeds would otherwise lose the ability to germinate, usually after a few decades. The CGIAR's rice gene bank at the International Rice Research Institute contains approximately 130,000 varieties and wild relatives; CIMMYT has over 100,000 types of wheat seed stored at a temperature of -18 degrees Celsius in a concrete silo in Mexico. All gene banks have fail-safe agreements with other institutions, to ensure there is always at least one set of back-up copies, and private and public gene banks collaborate extensively on the exchange of seeds and on salvage operations in the event of seeds being spoiled.

With about six hundred thousand accessions, the CGIAR system's gene banks are estimated to contain sample seeds of 40 percent of all developing-world crops, both cultivated and wild varieties. The CGIAR has entered into an agreement with the Food and Agriculture Organization of the United Nations that designates the gene banks as common global property. Although the task of handling the plant material still lies with the CGIAR, the current practice of free access for all to the holdings has now been ratified by an international agreement under which no special-interest groups receive any particular advantage.

In large areas of the developing world there is no great difference between the yields achieved by farmers and those on the research stations. The steady increase in yields year after year until 1990 does continue today, but the growth rate is lower while the population is still on the increase. Fortunately, though, this population trend is less marked today than in the 1960s and 1970s.[10] And at the research stations the signs indicate that getting much more mileage out of combining optimum farming techniques with the known plant material will be difficult. The yield gap is, to all intents and purposes, fixed.

Obviously, in such a situation the challenge for researchers and seed producers is to raise the yield ceiling. And although they are working hard to achieve this end, at both the national and international levels, some good working years have already been lost owing to a lack of funding.

The Danger of Overconfidence

Here we need to take a look back to the 1950s, when the Ford and Rockefeller foundations recognized that, with population growth outstripping growth in food production, something would have to be done to turn the tide. This realization triggered a research program that produced a number of improved varieties. Initially, this merely served to confirm the old adage that success breeds success. Most of the aid organizations and many governments in the developing world recognized the need to pull together, and much time and energy were invested in agricultural research and development. In the early 1980s the all-clear was sounded, signifying a job well done. By then, apart from isolated instances related to civil wars, famines no longer made the headlines.

This was the point at which the pattern of investment in developing-world agriculture and foreign aid in general did an about-turn. The ostensible success had engendered a certain degree of indifference: the problem of agricultural productivity had been sorted out; now there were other, more interesting items on the agenda. As a sign of this dwindling interest, development assistance to agricultural research and development dropped significantly.

The result was a shortfall in the production of research results that will take some time to make up. Maintenance research has just about managed to hold its own in most countries, but the real front-line research aimed at raising the yield ceiling has made no significant progress. And the research agenda has not, strictly speaking, been of much help either. The scant funds have—with good reason—gone toward developing many other aspects of farming techniques and plant varieties, rather than concentrating on increased yield potential alone. Once again Malthus's clash between population growth and food production looms threateningly on the horizon, particularly in Africa (see Chapter 3).

Meanwhile, the demand for dynamic food production has been extended to include concern for a number of other factors, mainly natural resources and environmental protection. Faced with the complexity of the problem, Malthus would surely have despaired. The one thing we cannot afford is to become passive members of his doomsayers' club.

2 • THE EXPANDING BOUNDARIES

OF RESEARCH   *Risks and Benefits*

Singapore has a wonderful zoo, with many exciting and un-usual attractions. For example, visitors can arrange to have break-fast with some amiable orangutans. A tourist who happened to turn fifty while visiting Singapore had breakfast at the zoo on his birthday and arranged for a photographer to take some shots of the birthday boy with a portly and thoughtful-looking orangutan on his lap. He sent the photos to friends and acquaintances with the inscription, "Celebrated my birthday with my closest relatives."

There is a lot more truth to this joke than one might think. Re-cent research not only has confirmed the strong similarities be-tween humans and apes (there's nothing new in that; every child knows that we "descended from the apes"), but also has found that if we delve down to the most minute level—down to an analysis of our genetic makeup—we find that up to 99 percent of the gene pool in human beings is exactly the same as that in the apes (orang-utans, gibbons, gorillas, and chimpanzees). Many of our genes and theirs seem to be identical.[1] So, in making comparisons at the gene-pool level (the gene pool being all the genes of all the individuals of a species that might interbreed), it is not the differences—although these are crucial—but the similarities that are most striking. The boundaries between the species are not necessarily as obvious or as hard and fast as we imagine.

New Insights

A brief digression is necessary here to look at some of the termi-nology involved in this latest biological discovery. The cells of all living things contain a complete set of those units, the *genes,* that determine the appearance and function of an organism. There are many genes in each cell, and the complement of genes varies from species to species. Each human cell contains about 30,000 genes, plant cells about 26,000, worm cells about 18,000, and yeast cells about 6,000.² Groups of genes are linked together in long chains called *chromosomes,* and each gene or chromosome carries out its functions singly or in conjunction with other genes and chromo-somes. The collective name for all the genes in all the chromo-somes of a species is the *genome.* (At the individual level, *genome* means all the genes in that particular organism.)

Genes function according to a hierarchy in which the heads of the genetic network are *regulator genes.* They determine the appear-ance and composition of a species and its control systems; for ex-ample, where the limbs develop on the body during embryonic de-velopment is controlled by these high-level genes. Genes on the lower rungs of the hierarchy are *functional genes.* For example, the function of a gene might be to contribute to the color of a plant's flowers.

In the past, it was assumed that for any species, the gene pool was constant throughout that species, but with slight variations from one individual to the next. The differences between individ-uals within a species manifest themselves both at the higher (regu-lator gene) level, in the appearance of the individual, and at the lower (functional gene) level, for example, in the production of substances that determine whether that individual will be healthy or not.

Constructing a complex table of the species, broken down into main divisions and subdivisions based on appearance and function, seemed, until recently, a logical way of categorizing living organ-isms. Species were seen as remaining fixed through time, with clear differences between one species and the next. A classification of flora, in which individual plants are defined according to leaf shape, root structure, appearance of the flower, number of stamens, and so forth, and arranged into families, is based on this understanding. The criteria for defining fauna led to whales being classified as mammals, not as fish, even though they live under water. For the higher species this method of classification is sound enough. New species have evolved very, very slowly over the ages, through genetic mutation and natural selection, and, generally, only beneficial changes that served to strengthen a species have been inherited and passed on. That, in a nutshell, is the Darwinian view of things.

We now know, however, that lower organisms such as bacteria do not have the same genetic stability as larger species but are continually changing into new forms. These changes only rarely occur through mutation: most commonly, change occurs when genes from one bacterium spontaneously transfer to another bacterium of a different species. Thus the notion of fixed boundaries on which the classification of species is founded has, on closer inspection, proven to be a fallacy.

This process of genetic mixing is also seen when bacteria attack and infect plants. For example, plants can be genetically modified by invading bacteria to produce "blisters" on their roots, so that the bacteria can feed on the host plant. New experimental research on mice suggests that genes from a virus that normally attacks bacteria can infiltrate the mouse's gene pool. Because the virus in question is quite foreign to the mouse's organs it does not affect their functioning, but an instance of "natural gene splicing" has in fact occurred. At the genetic level, mice resemble people, and it may well be that similar transferences are taking place all the time inside human bodies. If so, this has never led, as far as we can tell, to radical changes in humankind's appearance or function.

Mapping the Genome

The genetic similarities between species arise because all species are made up of identical "building blocks," put together in different ways. This also explains why genes can shift—or be shifted—between individuals of the same species and across those not so hard and fast species boundaries.

In practice, scientists already know how to bring about change in a species through traditional propagation, by crossing male and female flowers from different parents in a plant family. By crossing cultivated and wild plants, scientists have successfully produced some worthwhile hybrids. They have even cut across the established species categories to breed, for example, the cereal *triticale*, a hybrid of rye and wheat. With traditional propagation, clumps of genes are transferred, and only by observing the next generation of mature plants can one tell whether the desired combination has been achieved, one in which the best qualities of each parent have been passed on to a few of their offspring. And these qualities then must "breed true": must be passed on to the next and subsequent hybrid generations. Propagation by this method is a time-consuming process.

Although the number of genes involved is extremely large, scientists have come a long way in mapping the genomes of humans, other animals, plants, and lower organisms. They have produced complete maps of the genomes of certain bacteria and have made great strides in constructing a complete genetic picture of certain plants and animals regarded by the researchers as "model species." A worldwide project to compile a register of all human genes, the Human Genome Project, has now produced a draft description of the human genome, accomplished by two groups of researchers, one private, one public.

This book is predominantly concerned with the potential application of genetic modification in the propagation of farm crops. But genetic modification, or genetic engineering, is just one of the techniques collectively known as modern biotechnology (see Box 4)

Genetic Engineering in Traditional and Modern Plant Cultivation

Used in conjunction with conventional propagation techniques, the new discoveries in genetic engineering provide an excellent

BOX 4
BIOTECHNOLOGY

The term *biotechnology* covers all the techniques that use living organisms or substances from organisms to produce or alter a product, cause changes in plants or animals, or develop microorganisms for specific purposes. Modern biotechnology encompasses a number of techniques and methods. Advances in *molecular biology,* which underlies all these discoveries, have over the past sixty years allowed researchers to study the smallest, most basic units within the workings of the living cell. This has led to a completely new way of describing living organisms. A far cry from the old "schoolbook" method, based on appearance and function, this technology gets right down to the mapping of the genome, the complete set of genetic material in an individual organism. A number of techniques and methods play a key part in modern biotechnology.

- *Bioinformatics* is the name given to the presentation in a usable form of the data obtained from analysis of a genome, facilitating further work on these data.
- *Diagnostics* is the use of molecular characteristics in examining organisms. Diagnostics speeds up the process and improves the chances of locating pathogens and other foreign organisms, since there is no need to wait until the organism is fully developed and obviously infected.
- *Gene mapping* is the characterization of the genes, and the order in which they are linked, in chromosomes.
- *Gene splicing,* or *transformation,* is the transfer of one or more genes with certain prospectively useful qualities to plants, domestic animals, fish, or other organisms.
- *Molecular breeding* is an improved version of the conventional propagation of plants and animals. It locates and assesses qualities inherent in organisms, thus providing a more precise and quicker method—as early as the very first cell division in new hybrids—of selecting successful specimens for further development.

- *Tissue culture* is a means of growing tissues from single cells, manipulating them in various ways to produce the desired end products.
- *Vaccine technology* uses molecular biology as a means of and a short cut for developing modern vaccines.

tool for developing plants with various desirable characteristics. Even in the very earliest stages in the life of a new shoot, gene mapping can show whether the targeted combination of genes has been achieved. The desired new plant types are generated from individual cells by means of tissue culture, providing a large selection of cells for testing much earlier than with traditional culture methods. Researchers can also gain great advantages and save a great deal of time by using gene mapping to select parent plants most suitable for traditional breeding.

This is how things stand at the moment. Our knowledge about which genes carry which characteristics, and where these genes are located in the cell's genome, is growing rapidly. For lower-level genes, which act singly to perform simple functions, this knowledge can be applied in various ways:

- The genes already functioning within an organism can be altered; the effect of a particular gene can be suppressed or can be reinforced by increasing the number of gene copies in the cell. One example is the effect achieved by "shutting off" a gene that causes fast ripening of a fruit, making transportation of the fruit easier.
- A gene from one organism can be transferred to another organism of the same species. For example, a flavor gene from a wild tomato can be transferred to a cultivated tomato.
- A gene from one organism can be transferred to an organism of a quite different species. For example, the gene that enables mangrove trees to tolerate salt water can be transferred

to rice plants. This type of genetic modification is known as *transgenics* because it cuts across species.

- According to one theory, most organisms—all except the very simplest—contain in their genes a large number of biological attributes that have not been activated—that is, not all the genes are exerting their function.[3] If the nonactivated, or "silent," genes could be encouraged to interact with the organism's other genes, it might be possible to add certain desirable functions without having to go beyond species boundaries. For example, a potato could be endowed with the ability to withstand frost or with better taste or storability without bringing in genes from another species.

The technology behind the splicing of genes has been developed by observing and applying the biological processes involved in nature's own gene splicing. The first successfully executed experiment, carried out in 1972 in the United States, entailed cutting a gene out of one organism and joining it to a chromosome of another. Denmark was quick to adopt the process, first in the pharmaceutical industry: human insulin for the treatment of diabetes was prepared from genetically manipulated microorganisms contained in closed tanks, rather than being obtained from livestock. In 1994 the first GM plant product appeared on supermarket shelves in the United States: a slower-ripening tomato. Although, from the manufacturer's point of view, this seemed an excellent idea, it was not a great moneymaker. Since then, however, other products have been a runaway success.

One can use various techniques to isolate a gene from an organism. The gene can be "tied to" the genetic material of a bacterium, then attached to this pair is a gene that will be easy to spot in the later stages of the process—what is known as a *marker gene*. This "gene pack" is then propagated to form numerous identical copies.

The isolated gene now has to be transferred to the organism in which it is intended to function. To be reproduced by the organism—that is, to be handed down to the next generation—the gene must find its way into the egg or sperm cells. Here, again, there are a number of options from which to choose. The gene can be tied to a bacterium of the type that naturally splices itself to the roots of plants without harming the organism. The new gene is then transported through the cell wall and eventually joins the plant's other genes in its genome. Or, one can shoot the gene into the cell with a *gene gun*, which has microscopic bullets into which the gene has been inserted. These bullets function exactly like a bacterium, boring through the cell wall.

These techniques do not, by any means, work every time, and splicing new genes into an organism with the technology currently in use is a job requiring great patience. The marker gene hooked up to the transferred gene is used to check whether the splicing has been successful.

Weighing the Risks to Human Health

This brings us to the heart of one of the problems with the new technology. A standard method of identifying a genetically modified cell in the laboratory has been by means of a marker gene that endows the cell with resistance to an antibiotic. If that antibiotic is added to the gene recipients in the gene modification experiment, only those organisms containing the marker gene—and thus the gene the experimenter wanted to transfer—will survive. This works well for experimental purposes. But if the marker gene injected with the gene pack into a plant remains part of that plant, in the next and subsequent generations, from then on that plant will be resistant to antibiotics (as are many bacteria, for example). While there is no evidence of this causing problems for the people or animals that eat the plant, the possibility that this resistance will be passed on cannot be totally discounted. The antibiotic-resistance marker was chosen because it was easy for researchers to work with in the laboratory, but they have lived to regret their choice.

There are a number of ways to resolve this dilemma, the obvious one being to develop other types of marker genes. Researchers in a number of countries have succeeded in developing harmless markers based on carbohydrates that occur naturally in plant and human cells,4 and other research groups are well on their way to developing other kinds of markers. Another way of solving the problem would be to remove the marker once the gene transfer has taken place, and this technique is now in use.

The transfer technique itself is another debatable point. Genetic modification is a very precise technique compared with conventional propagation, in which genes are transferred in indiscriminant clumps. On this point scientists generally agree. But its precision is limited, inasmuch as the transferred gene is randomly placed in the chromosome of the recipient organism, with no way of knowing in advance exactly how it will interact with the thousands of other genes of that organism's genome. One might say that this has always been the way when crossbreeding plants, and new varieties have always been tried out in laboratories and test fields for long periods before researchers claim with certainty that the plants are functioning as expected. Over several growing seasons, the new varieties must show they have new, advantageous qualities that are uniform and consistent from one generation to the next.

The safety measures established for GM crops are far more exacting than those for new varieties of plants propagated by traditional methods. The first step after modification is to carry out growing trials in protected greenhouses, where plants are tested for, among other things, various constituent substances and allergens, according to stringent standards laid down by the authorities. In the case of countries within the European Union, these are joint E.U. standards. In the United States, the Environmental Protection Agency, the Department of Agriculture, and the Food and Drug Administration are responsible for various components of the standards. Basically, the test procedures work from the initial premise that the new plants are just like the old familiar ones except in that one isolated area where the aim has been to make a change.

If the isolation trials proceed without a hitch and the desired result—and no other result—is achieved, the authorities may give permission for trials on test plots, in order to assess the plant's performance and its compatibility with the surrounding fields and countryside. If these trials also go well, scientists may seek permission to try out the plant on farmland. If permission is granted, the plant undergoes a trial period of seven years. In most European countries companies have not yet reached the stage of selling GM seeds to farmers. Within the European Union, permission has been granted for the production of GM plants in only a few cases; only limited quantities of such crops are being grown at the moment. Permission has also been given to import products or raw materials produced with the help of GM plants into E.U. member countries. In the United States, permission to commercialize GM seed has been granted for several commodities and production is already widespread.

It is generally agreed that such strict authorization procedures are well worthwhile, and a number of mistakes have been picked up through this process. The most famous example is the case of the soybeans that were given a gene from Brazil nuts in order to boost the oil content of the beans. Brazil nuts, however, cause an allergic reaction in some people. Fortunately, the researchers were aware of this possible side effect and performed tests to see whether the allergen was passed on to the soybeans. When they found that it was, greenhouse trials were discontinued, even though the soybeans were developed to be used only as animal fodder. To some, this demonstrates that the safety measures work. Others, however, point to this as an example of the risks involved in the genetic modification of crops for human consumption.

The safety measures appear to be well warranted, if only on the basis of the amount of concern generated by GM crops. Yet the amount of normal variation in the constituent substances of all crops has never attracted much attention. As one researcher put it, "It might be quite interesting to carry out comparable analyses of conventionally grown, organically grown, and genetically modified cultivated plants. Although such studies can be very expensive and the question is, do we really need such information?"[5] An American researcher involved in the authorization process for GM crops is even more categorical in his assessment: "The allergy tests are so extensive that most of our foodstuffs would never pass them."[6]

The point that both researchers are making—while in no way disagreeing with the safety requirements placed on GM crops—is that, as far as they can see, even without advanced screening systems, conventional and organic farming do not appear to have done any noticeable harm to people's health.

The Poisoned Rat Debate

The debate surrounding the health question flared up once again at the end of 1998 and burned fiercely through the first half of 1999, after the results of experiments carried out by Dr. Arpad Pusztai, a researcher at a government-funded institute in Scotland, were made public. Pusztai thought his findings on the effects of GM potatoes on rats represented such conclusive proof of the dangers of genetic modification that, contrary to standard scientific practice, he released his interim findings to the press.[7] Over the next few days, the affair escalated into something of a public scandal when Pusztai was first complimented on his work, then suspended by his employer. The institute was widely accused of a miscarriage of justice, on the grounds that Pusztai was fired not because he released his findings prematurely but because his negative findings on GM crops could make things awkward for the government and private companies. After reviewing all the documentation, the research institute where Pusztai was employed issued a statement to the effect that it found his conclusions unsound and publication of his interim findings irresponsible.

In Pusztai's experiments, a substance found in snowdrops that provides this flowering plant with defense against insects was integrated into potatoes, in an attempt to endow them with a similar resistance to insects—without, of course, rendering the potatoes toxic to animals or people. The resulting GM potatoes were then fed to laboratory rats. When inconsistencies were detected in the effects on the rats' organs and growth, which apparently could not be attributed solely to the presence of toxins, the conclusion was that the genetic modification itself had caused the damage.

Prompted by these disturbing reports, the prestigious British scientific body, the Royal Society, set up a committee of inquiry, which spent some months examining the research material from all angles. In the spring of 1999, the committee's findings were published in a report that criticized the quality of the work and many of the techniques used. It found no foundation for arriving at any conclusions based on that study.[8] Subsequently, when Pusztai's material was published in a scientific journal,[9] the journal's scientific advisers protested indignantly that they did not understand how an article of such poor quality could have slipped through the usual safety net provided by the peer-review process—comments from experts in the field. One British critique also pointed out that if a GM product had shown the effects suggested in these alarming reports, it would have been weeded out in the course of the screening process and would never have got beyond the laboratory stage.[10]

Weighing the Risks to the Environment

The health aspect is only one side of the debate on the legitimacy of genetic modification in agriculture. Another line of argument concerns how the new plants will function in the field and how they will fit in with the surrounding environment, whether cultivated land or wild countryside. These are problems one needs to consider in many aspects of modern-day plant propagation; they are not unique to GM plants. The problems are formulated either as general questions about the end products of the new technology or as specific queries about the few plants that have so far been developed and made widely available in a number of countries.

The purpose of propagating GM plants, from a scientific point of view, is the same as that of propagating plants by existing methods: to create new plant material providing better quality and higher yields at lower cost. Until now, this has mostly been interpreted as meaning lower costs to farmers. As a result the emphasis in industrialized agriculture has been on two positive attributes of the new plants: simpler weed control and less expenditure on spraying with pesticides. These benefits have, by and large, shaped the debate on the effects on the environment.

Weed Control

Researchers have identified a number of wild plants endowed with a natural resistance to chemicals that plants cannot normally withstand. The resistance gene from these species has been transferred to crops such as maize, soybeans, turnips, cotton, and rape. When farmers sow the GM plants, they can spray their fields with weed-killing chemicals without harming the crop.

Several companies have developed new plants of this type—the same companies that produce the universal weed killers, or *herbicides,* that the plants are designed to withstand. For example, the multinational company Monsanto manufactures the herbicide Roundup and also markets herbicide resistant maize, beet, and rape seeds under the brand name Roundup Ready. The seeds and chemicals go hand in hand: there is little sense in one without the other. What is so special about this first generation of GM crops is that the genes are integrated into varieties that the farmers already know to be reliable, so the GM version is chosen purely because it makes the work of farming easier and cheaper.

Roundup and similar herbicides produced by other companies are chosen for this strategy because they degrade rapidly and therefore are often considered among the most acceptable agricultural chemicals. And indeed, when this type of weed killer first appeared on the market as a standard herbicide, it was hailed as a step in the right direction environmentally—replacing, as it did, some much more noxious chemicals. Householders who wanted to spray their driveways with weed killer felt they could now do it with a good conscience, using these new, milder herbicides. More recently, however, the general attitude toward the long-term effects of using herbicides in any shape or form has been more guarded, a feeling that has rubbed off on GM plant technology.

If we look at the question of toxicity alone, we can see some advantages to be gained from GM crops as opposed to those grown by traditional methods. For traditional crops, the soil has to be thoroughly prepared before sowing to help prevent weed seeds from germinating. During the growing season, the plants must be sprayed with several different herbicides, each of which takes care of particular kinds of weeds without harming the crop. Genetically modified crops require less intensive soil preparation, and weeds can be left to germinate and grow for a while, before the farmer needs to administer a dose of herbicide appropriate to the size of the weed problem. The burgeoning weeds are good for helpful insects, birds, and small mammals. And because the herbicide falls on a dense cover of weeds rather than on newly prepared soil, the chance of toxins leaching into the soil is reduced. A controlled study of GM turnips cultivated in test fields on farms, carried out by the Danish National Environmental Research Institute, was actually titled "GM Turnips Benefit the Environment."[11] The study found that where farmers let the weeds grow somewhat before spraying the fields, they used 50 percent less herbicide than with traditional weeding. And there was no drop whatever in the turnip yield. These tests confirmed what had already been seen in the greenhouse phase of GM turnip cultivation.

This aspect of the effect of these herbicides on the environment does not appear to present any great problem, and in any case this is not the main area of concern about potential environmental harm—although the latest findings on yields may well have come as something of a surprise to critics of this type of GM plant. The main point at issue is the possible dispersal of the plants' genetically engineered properties to their wild cousins. We return to this topic later in the chapter.

Resistance to Insects

The bacterium *Bacillus thurengiensis* (Bt for short), a widely distributed species with many variants, produces a mild toxin that acts on a small selection of insects harmful to a number of crops. This toxin presents no known danger to insects that do not pose problems for agriculture or that actually help production by pollinating cultivated plants.

The virtues of Bt have been known for many years. Even organic farmers spray Bt on their fields when insect attacks get out of hand. Because it is produced naturally, biodegrades rapidly, and has no known harmful side effects, it is recognized as a permissible pesticide for use in otherwise nontoxic farming. Genetic engineering enables farmers to apply Bt to crops directly and automatically, by integrating the ability to produce the toxin into the plants themselves. International seed-producing companies have already successfully developed several Bt-producing crops, including maize, cotton, and tomatoes.

On the face of it, this seems like a major step forward. After all, if crops have their own specific built-in resistance to pests, farmers do not need to use the universal pesticides that are the norm in conventional agriculture. But critics still find it hard to see the advantages. There is all the difference in the world, they say, between intermittent spraying with the Bt toxin and a constant level of Bt in the plants. Spraying with Bt reduces the pest population, but a proportion of it will survive. For large populations of insects, there is no great danger that the handful of insects that develop a resistance to Bt will meet, mate, and pass on their resistance to future generations. The inherent effect of constant exposure to Bt, however, would be a drastic reduction in the insect population, which would increase the chances of surviving individuals breeding and passing on resistance. This natural selection of the best-adapted individuals, as we know, forms the basis for Darwin's concept of "survival of the fittest." Such a development—a highly likely one, in the long term—could mean that at some point organic farming would have to manage without the Bt toxin. But Bt, as we have noted, has many variants; farmers could switch to a different variant, if necessary, as is regularly done for other substances with "worn-out" properties in conventional plant production.

The problem of resistant insects can be minimized by setting up regulations for how farming is to be conducted. Such regulations are already in force in the United States, where farmers are required to provide refuges—reserved areas—for insects. This may mean setting aside areas where crop spraying is kept to a minimum or planting a certain proportion of a crop as non-GM varieties. This would limit toxic concentrations and reduce the risk of resistance, or at least postpone it, depending on the size of the areas set aside as refuges. At the beginning of 2000, U.S. federal authorities tightened the rules in this area, which far too many farmers were managing to circumvent one way or another.

The shift to Bt from standard chemicals is packed with potential. In China over the past four years, a large share of the traditional cotton varieties have been supplanted by Bt varieties. No statistics are available on the impact of this shift at the national level, but in Hebei Province about one million farmers are now growing Bt cotton. Given that cotton grown by conventional methods is extremely vulnerable to pests, cotton growers depend heavily on pesticides. The transition to the Bt varieties in China has resulted in an 80 percent reduction in pesticide use on fields planted with Bt cotton. In addition, conditions for all insect life are so much improved that the pests that prey on cotton are now more likely to be attacked by their natural enemies, whose numbers have increased by 25 percent.[12]

The Endangered Butterfly

Alarming interim research findings on Bt crops were made public in a report that was expected to deal a decisive blow to the future of the new Bt technology. In May 1999 a team of American researchers reported that when they fed monarch caterpillars with pollen from Bt maize in their laboratories, the caterpillars were seriously damaged and many died. Because one supposed advantage of the Bt technique was that it was not harmful to friendly insects, and because the subject of the experiment was the picturesque monarch butterfly, a huge outcry ensued, led by an alliance of environmental organizations and the press. As we noted in the Introduction, the matter caused a great furor in the United States. It even had political repercussions in Europe, where approval of several GM plants up for authorization was put on hold (see Chapter 6).

This affair was treated somewhat differently from Pusztai's potato experiments, because the laboratory experiment had been handled in a scientifically sound manner, but—as the researchers conceded—this laboratory research could yield only limited results, which needed to be expanded. This was done over the summer and autumn through various field experiments. The conclusions—which, as it happens, have not received much media exposure—allayed fears about the well-being of the monarch butterfly and other friendly insects.

In the laboratory, feeding conditions for the monarch caterpillars were unnatural, inasmuch as the caterpillars had nothing to eat but the pollen from the Bt maize, for which they have no particular preference. In the wild, monarch caterpillars live almost exclusively on milkweed. This plant can be found growing near fields of maize, but for the most part, maize pollen does not travel many feet away from the plant (and a high concentration of pollen would be needed to reach a level harmful to the caterpillars), and the leaves of the milkweed are so smooth that, even if maize pollen did land on them, they would not retain much of it. Researchers also pointed out that the weaker caterpillars, which might be expected to be the most likely to succumb to Bt-infected pollen, live on the underside of the milkweed leaves, where the pollen does not land. And lastly, of all the climate belts in North America where monarch butterflies can be found, in only a handful of areas are the butterflies at the caterpillar stage at the same time that maize is shedding its pollen.[13] So, in this instance, neither the monarch butterfly nor any other friendly insects seem to be in imminent danger.

The attention given to this particular case contrasts strangely with the general attitude toward standard agricultural practices: conventional pesticides, which do not differentiate between friend and foe, kill a great many harmless insects. The fierce denunciation of clearly targeted and contained pest control through Bt plants is perhaps a little out of touch with reality. In all probability, more butterflies survive near Bt fields than near those sprayed with conventional pesticides.

The Fear of Gene Dispersal

Genetically modified crops have been likened to plants and animals introduced into an area from some other part of the world, whether by accident or design. The most notorious example of this was the introduction of rabbits into Australia, where in certain regions they became a downright plague. And sometimes the unwelcome intrusion is much more local. In Great Britain, for example, certain varieties of rhododendron are considered a thing of beauty in the garden and stubborn weeds on the other side of the garden fence. On the benefit side, one could point to the introduction to European agriculture of wheat and potatoes and other vegetables and flowers, brought in by accident. Moving live organisms from one place to another can cause problems, but sometimes there is much to be gained.

Today, though, strict limitations and quarantine regulations govern the importation of seeds, live animals, and growing plants. No country or region would knowingly import a new crop without careful analysis of its quality, its adaptability to local conditions, its state of health, and its compatibility with other plant and animal life. National authorities' analysis of GM plants is based on just these sorts of considerations, supplemented by new requirements and backed up by modern high-tech testing techniques.

The close kinship between GM crops and existing plants, however, gives rise to another worry: the risk of inadvertent mingling of the old and the new. This fear is founded on an awareness of the normal way in which many agricultural crops (and all flowering plants) are propagated, through cross-pollination.

Quite a catalog can be drawn up of the possible pitfalls of GM plants both for existing agriculture and the surrounding countryside. An abbreviated list runs like this:

- Pollen from GM plants could fertilize neighboring, non-GM plants. Organically grown crops and their seeds would thus be "polluted."
- The modified gene could be dispersed to wild relatives, and these weeds (superweeds, as they are called) would benefit from the attribute added to the GM plant.
- Seeds dropped by the GM plant might survive in the field and shoot up the following season as a troublesome weed.

There is nothing new about any of these scenarios. They are no different from those occurring in conventional plant propagation, where the aim is also to improve the plants in one or more particular aspects. These plants also cross-pollinate with close and not so close relatives, because that is how flowering plants reproduce.

Why has this interplay between cultivated farmland and wild countryside, between one field and the next, never before been a common concern? The reason is that cultivated varieties are seldom robust enough to survive without help from the farmer in the form of soil preparation, weed control, fertilization of fields, and so on. The specific agricultural properties bred into cultivated plants rarely give them a competitive edge in the wild, which explains why there is no sign of superweeds in the fields. The properties that GM material can bring to weeds would be of only limited benefit to these plants. A weed's ability to withstand a pesticide in the wild is clearly of use to the plant only if the spot where it grows is sprayed with that pesticide.

Some Positive Attributes of Genetic Modification

Public attention has, with good reason, been focused on GM plants that can withstand herbicides and manage without pesticides. It is on these that most research time and effort has been invested, and the results have been staggering.

Farmers in the United States welcomed the new technologies with open arms, and the three main GM crops—maize, soybeans, and rape—captured between 25 and 50 percent of the seed market in the last three years of the 1990s. Canada and Argentina are hard on the United States' heels, particularly with maize and soybeans, and Mexico and South Africa now have a measure of GM crop output under way. The big unknown quantity is China. The actual figures are regarded as state secrets, but statistics for certain crops such as tobacco and cotton in some provinces indicate that China is investing all its energies in the switch to GM crops. The first GM rice plants will probably soon be appearing in its farmers' fields.[14]

The task facing the major seed-producing companies has clearly been to make the farmer's work easier, to reduce production costs, and to recoup the money invested in research. And so far they have been pretty successful in this. But part of their aim has also been to reduce the level of toxic residue in agricultural products—not down to the level achieved by organic farming but enough to produce a genuine improvement that would set consumers' minds at ease. One great spin-off from this easier, cheaper farming is that the pressure has to some extent—and in certain areas to a great extent—been taken off the environment. This is also an obvious advantage for consumers. But the more recent GM agricultural products already perfected or in the pipeline appear to offer benefits quite different from those seen in the first wave of GM products.

One advantage that tends to be overlooked—and is of primary interest to us here—is the increase in yield. More work is being done on this front, either directly, by rendering plants more productive so that they yield more or larger seeds or fruit, or indirectly, by limiting losses, which, particularly in developing countries, can mean the difference between a potential and an actual harvest.

Through genetic modification, science now has the facility to combine properties so that plants capable of withstanding weed killers *and* combating insects from within will soon be a reality. One such plant is a potato that repels the Colorado beetle, which can completely destroy a potato crop. Scientists have also been able to produce plants resistant to many agricultural pests and diseases through conventional propagation, but the techniques employed up to now have been of no help in dealing with most viral infections. Nor can viruses be combated by spraying. Genetic modification has led to a breakthrough in this field, producing the first plants with a built-in resistance to viruses.

Conventional propagation techniques have also brought us a long way in improving the quality of individual crops and developing vastly different characteristics in various strains of the same crop; for example, they have produced wheat varieties that are better for producing baking flour or for making pasta. And conventional technology has made great strides in improving the yield of plants under difficult farming conditions, say with limited rainfall or in soil with an adverse chemical makeup.

Dramatic improvements have also been made in the ability of plants to get the most out of the nutrients in the soil. For example, the capacity of wheat to extract nutrients from the soil has increased so much that, with the best varieties and good farming know-how, farmers can now apply one-fifth of the traditional amount of nitrogen fertilizer without any drop in yield. In the 1950s and early 1960s, tall varieties of wheat required almost 400 kilograms of nitrogen to produce a yield of 5 tons. This has gradually been reduced to about 75 kilograms of nitrogen for the varieties developed in the mid-1980s.[15] The possibility for reducing the need for fertilizer is also important environmentally. In industrialized and some developing countries, excess chemical fertilizer sometimes leaches into the groundwater, damaging the water supply. And in developing countries, the limited amounts of organic fertilizer available, such as green and animal manure, would stretch farther with more nutrition-efficient crops.

Other positive results of genetic modification are improvements in the characteristics of certain varieties of plants. The first varieties of rapeseed with an oil content healthier for consumers are already appearing on the market. Sweeter tomatoes and strawberries have been perfected, as well as potatoes with a higher starch content. Such products can provide consumers in the developed world with some new choices from an already abundant range of fruit and vegetables—assuming, of course, that there is a demand for these goods.

A concentrated effort is also being made to improve qualities of particular interest in developing countries. The typical diet of the poor in a developing country is often unbalanced, with grains and root vegetables the main ingredients in their daily fare. When this diet is only rarely supplemented by green vegetables or meat, people suffer from a lack of vitamins and other micronutrients. The use of food supplements such as vitamin pills to make up the deficit, as do people in the West, is not a practical solution for the poor in the developing countries; such supplements are too expensive and often difficult to distribute in rural areas. So researchers in public research institutes, national and international, are working toward breeding crops with a higher content of the nutrients that are missing.

A fair amount of progress has been made, using traditional techniques, toward increasing the iron content in grain crops such as rice, maize, and wheat, which are absolutely central to the daily diet in most developing countries. Work is also being carried out on beans and cassava. In these plants as well as the grains, researchers are examining ways of improving their zinc, vitamin A, and iron content. Their findings have been promising, but until recently they have had to look at these nutrients one at a time. Because no known variety of rice plant contains a high level of vitamin A, for example, researchers cannot develop vitamin A–enriched rice through traditional methods such as crossbreeding. In an exciting research breakthrough, using genetic modification techniques scientists have now incorporated beta-carotene (converted into vitamin A in the human body), as well as more iron, into rice in the laboratory. But a lot more work needs to be done on this, because the type of rice used in the experiments is easy to work with but not particularly common, and the flavor and appearance of the new rice leave something to be desired. Nevertheless, this project shows that ongoing work using genetic modification can produce important benefits for both farmers and consumers.

On other fronts, efforts are under way to develop plants that can survive on less water and on soils with a naturally high content of metals such as aluminum, as occurs in large stretches of savannah in Africa and South America. A breakthrough here could open up vast areas of land for grain cultivation. In the long run, this would not only increase crop production but also ease the strain on over-cultivated slopes and hillsides. As we mentioned earlier, another ongoing project is to develop a rice that can cope with saltwater flooding, by inserting genes from salt-tolerant mangrove trees that grow in coastal regions in the tropics.

Leguminous plants have the ability to convert, or "fix," nitrogen in the air into ammonia and nitrate, both of which are absorbed and used by plants. This boosts the nutritional content of both soil and crops. If farmers plant legumes such as peas or beans and leave the roots in the soil after harvesting, they need much less chemical fertilizer or manure for their next crop. Farmers also capitalize on this attribute by planting other crops—annuals, shrubs, or trees—alongside the legumes and by rotating the crops on each field from year to year—an ancient farming practice. Years of work in the van-guard of international public research have been invested in at-tempting to transfer the nitrogen-fixing ability of legumes into grain crops. This has been an agricultural researcher's dream, though not always easy to believe in. There are tremendous ben-efits to be gained, both environmental and economic, from any ad-vances made in this field. While genetic engineering is unlikely to solve this problem in the very near future, the new techniques do allow the work to be much more focused.

Australian researchers have made great progress in creating plants that produce vaccine against the most common children's diseases.[16] A measles vaccine produced in tobacco leaves has suc-cessfully been tried out on mice, which developed immunity within just a few weeks. Experiments with monkeys are now being planned. The next stage would be to grow "vaccine fruit" in the greenhouse, thereby making vaccination programs cheaper and more effective, especially in the developing countries, where hy-

giene and the storage of vaccines and syringes can be major problems.

When we look at these advances, once considered scientific long
shots, it no longer seems like pie in the sky to think that, at some
point in the future, biotechnology could produce plants that make
more efficient use of solar energy—which is, after all, the driving
force behind plants' conversion of nutrients into the raw ingredients of our diet. The efficiency with which sunlight is used can
vary considerably from plant to plant, and there can be a big difference in the amount of damage done to various plant species by inadequate sunlight when the temperature is low, which sets the
limit for how far north or south of the equator a plant can be
grown. Some plants, such as bamboo, spring up so fast you can almost hear them grow. Seaweeds and other algae that grow under
water where sunlight is filtered and diffused have the capacity to
make the most of the light available. If this capacity could be transferred from algae to plants, it would do a great deal for productivity in both industrialized and developing countries.

Genetic modification can realistically be expected to benefit developing countries in at least three ways: first, by increasing productivity, right down to the smallholder level of agriculture; second, and every bit as important, by reducing vulnerability to the
whims of nature; and third, by improving the nutritional quality of
the food. These three improvements not only will be of help to
each farming family, no matter how small the farm, but also are of
vital importance to the entire rural village society, keeping in mind
that 70 percent of the poor in developing countries live in rural
areas. Granted, a large steady supply of food makes for lower
prices, but since the farmer's cost per unit will also drop, this
means larger overall profits and a better living both for those growing solely for their own needs and for those with something to take
to market.

Some of these futuristic possibilities depend on scientists being
able to locate whole groups of genes—not just a single gene—that
govern a particular quality, and complex tasks of this sort will ob-

viously take time. But the most remarkable thing in genetic engineering, as in other recent advances in science and technology such as information technology, is probably the speed at which new discoveries and their practical application have happened—much faster than the fathers of the science, and even its most avid enthusiasts, could have expected.

3 · WHAT IS WRONG WITH MORE OF THE SAME?

It is the end of the nineteenth century. In a poor Danish farm family, everyone should have been in bed long ago, but no one can sleep on this November night. The atmosphere is tense, and no one has much to say. The mother, whose eyes are wet, is being comforted by a neighbor's wife. The children huddle together fearfully on the benches lining the walls of the living room. Father is over in the barn, tending the ailing pig, which they bought in the spring to fatten up. It is the family's only resource. Through the summer and fall, the pig has been tended carefully and fed better than anyone in the family: its slaughter is the family's guarantee of getting through the winter with at least a little meat on their bones. Desperate prayers for mercy are sent up, but the pig does not make it through the night. The outlook for the little family is bleak.

This tragedy is recounted in the short story "Deathblow," by the Danish writer Henrik Pontoppidan.[1] Over a hundred years later, this story can still make a Dane's blood run cold. Few people outside Denmark know Pontoppidan's name. And even in his native land it is doubtful whether many still read the stories in which he depicted the lives of poor farming families with such poignancy that the public indignation he aroused helped trigger major social reforms.

Stories like Pontoppidan's seldom attract much attention in the industrialized world today, but the need for them is just as great. Millions of families in developing countries are every bit as vulnerable today as was Pontoppidan's smallholder family, and they are struck by similar, staggering deathblows. The situation for these people is dire, and yet this massive tragedy does not give rise to much comment or any widespread concern in the industrialized countries. After all, things are going just fine—aren't they?

Keeping Disaster More or Less at Bay

There are many ways of depicting the reality of the developing countries. The media usually opt to report on the rare sensational occurrences—disastrous crop failures, floods, earthquakes, famine relief, airlifts—events that are straightforward and clear-cut, no matter how overwhelming they may be to those on the spot. These, though, are out-of-the-ordinary situations, and newspaper readers and television viewers in Europe and North America might assume that before and after these crises, everyday life is well-ordered and reasonably okay.

Relief organizations make their appeals on the same terms: things have gone terribly wrong somewhere in the world and something must be done, fast, to restore the status quo. It may take time, and much rebuilding may have to be done, but we are given the feeling that once things are back to the way they were before the disaster occurred, the end will have been achieved.

The disaster reports we receive from developing countries are not the whole picture. Some private groups and official development organizations—and to some extent the media—do a sterling job of tirelessly reporting on day-to-day life, the problems faced, and successes achieved in the poor countries of the world. But, though readily available, this information never seems to make a great impact on the general public. In any case, one gets the impression that while the people may be poor, as long as there are no civil wars or floods or other natural disasters, life will follow its simple quiet course in the villages of the developing world. We are not seeing the appalling famines in such heavily populated countries as Bangladesh, China, and India that were considered inevitable twenty-five to thirty years ago. And for certain countries and regions where the situation seemed worse than hopeless, some international debaters cynically suggested that we stop supporting these regions, since there were so many other tasks to be addressed where success was more likely. Nature should just be allowed to take its course. But this judgment was too harsh to be adopted as policy and, as we saw in Chapter 2, efforts to improve food production in the developing countries produced some excellent results.

The threat of disaster faded, and since then any serious problems with the food supply in developing countries seemed to be merely a momentary hiccup. Though these countries may be poor, things seem to be going reasonably well for them on the food front.

The Silent Hunger

If a Pontoppidan of our own day was looking for an equally dire real-life story to tell, he would have no difficulty in finding farming families on the brink of tragedy. He would only have to travel to Africa or South Asia, where the largest numbers of the world's hungry people live. These people go to bed hungry and wake up to so little daily food that their stomachs never feel full. Their numbers are so large that we cannot grasp them: 820 million people—several times the population of the United States—have too little to eat every day.[2]

We can illustrate this situation with cold, clear statistics. In sub-Saharan Africa, the average food intake is roughly 2,100 calories per person per day, far too low an average by anyone's calculations. In South Asia, which includes the many millions of inhabitants in the heavily populated countries of Bangladesh, India, and Pakistan, the average is about 2,400 calories per person—which would be all right if everybody got it, but as an average it is too low. Those who live in the industrialized countries eat very well—an average of about 3,250 calories a day. The difference between that and the average in the developing world is grotesque.[3]

Too few calories does not simply mean that people are thin. In the long run, not having enough to eat has a harmful effect on children's growth and intellectual development and on the immune system. A deficit of calories hits children particularly hard because they are doubly vulnerable: not only do they have too little to eat every day during childhood, but if their mothers were undernourished during pregnancy, the children were probably underweight at birth. One-third of all children under five in the developing countries are below the size of well-nourished children of that age group. The implications for their future are severe. And again, Africa and South Asia are heavily overrepresented in these statistics.[4]

Undernourishment and malnourishment result in adults who do not have the energy to do their day-to-day work and children who are less active and less open to learning. Malnourished people are more susceptible to diseases. It does not take much for an undernourished child to succumb to what would be a trivial illness in a well-fed child. The dire situation in Pontoppidan's Danish smallholding may be repeated, even more desperately, in many a mud-walled home in India, where the family's prayers are not for an ailing pig but for the recovery of a sickly, coughing child or for rain before the crop is lost. As Pontoppidan points out in his story, in his heart of hearts the Danish smallholder finds it hard to believe that God would go so far as to take the family pig: "Better then—if ill luck should befall—that he took one of the children. For what would they do if the pig were to die?" Such terrible dilemmas are still faced by desperate souls on smallholdings in some parts of the world every day.

"Hidden Hunger"

As shocking as these figures are, another tragedy lurks behind them—one of the world's better-kept secrets. The effects of malnutrition are clearly visible when we are brought face to face with emaciated road workers in India or hollow-cheeked, apathetic babies in Malawi. What is not so apparent is that all these millions of underfed people, and many more besides, also suffer from another form of malnutrition, which is why researchers talk of "hidden hunger."

The problem is lack of an adequate supply of micronutrients—minerals and vitamins—in the daily diet. Many poor people in developing countries eat a very unbalanced diet, consisting mainly of boiled rice or maize porridge—good foods, as far as they go, and filling. But unless they are supplemented by fruits, vegetables, and fish or meat, the body will develop a deficiency of the vital nutrients necessary to make it strong and keep it healthy.

One cannot go without the most essential micronutrients (for example, iron, zinc, iodine, and vitamin A) for any length of time without serious ill effects. Iron is vital for ensuring an adequate supply of blood cells (blood count) and, consequently, the circulation of oxygen around the body. With a balanced diet, or one backed up by vitamin and mineral supplements, the body's blood count generally remains stable. For those of us who live in the rich parts of the world, if someone loses blood or the iron content of the blood declines for some reason, it can soon be built up again with iron supplementation, so we rarely give this a second thought. We take it for granted that the iron content in our blood will be "normal"—that is, appropriate to the body's need for iron. But if one looks at the blood iron content of people around the world, it seems that *we* are the ones who are abnormal. Of the six billion people in the world, five billion are iron-deficient, two billion to such a degree that they suffer from anemia. Women and children are particularly prone to iron deficiency. Women find it difficult to replace the blood lost in menstruation and childbirth. In regions such as Southeast Asia, three-quarters of the women and two-thirds of the children are anemic.[5] A serious lack of iron has just as debilitating an effect on the immune system as does undernutrition and often leads to retardation in children and reduced working capacity in adults.

Vitamin A deficiency reduces the body's resistance to infectious diseases. Recent research shows a strong link between vitamin A deficiency and the severity of HIV/AIDS. Studies show that an adequate supply of vitamin A, largely found in fruits, vegetables, and meat, could reduce the child mortality rate by as much as 20 percent in the developing countries where the deficiency is most prevalent. Around the world, 125 million children show symptoms of vitamin A deficiency, and as a result 14 million have seriously impaired vision or blindness. As long as the deficiency is not pronounced, it remains hidden and can be detected only by blood tests.[6]

Other forms of dietary deficiency also can cause illness and physical impairment, making life grim and often short for many inhabitants of developing countries. According to recent estimates, every day forty thousand people die of illnesses related to their poor diet.[7]

Where Do We Go from Here?

Enough calories are produced by the world's agriculture to cover the energy requirements of every person in the world today. Statistics show that every single one of us on this earth could be receiving our quota of 2,750 calories per day. As we have seen, though, this is only a theoretical average: many millions of people survive—if they do—on much less. Statistical averages won't fill their bellies. Essential foods need to be available close to where people live, and they need to be affordable.

The required amount of daily calories forms the basis for estimating how much food is needed to feed the world now and in the future. Such estimates help answer the question of what needs to be done if the situation is to improve by the time children born today reach adulthood. The International Food Policy Research Institute has developed an analytical model and carried out a series of studies that project what the world food situation will look like up to the year 2020.[8] These analyses, along with proposals for a goal-oriented local and global effort to eliminate poverty and hunger, have been incorporated into a program known as the 2020 Vision for Food, Agriculture, and the Environment.

The 2020 Vision scenarios are based on IFPRI's own research

and on data supplied by a string of international organizations working in such areas as nutrition, population growth, agricultural production, market conditions, prices of major export crops, and various aspects of policy. Other organizations, such as the Food and Agriculture Organization of the United Nations (FAO) and the World Bank, have developed similar models based on somewhat shorter or longer time frames and with prognoses showing slightly different figures. But the general trends remain the same from one model to the next.

The 2020 Vision program looks at the various dynamic factors that will affect worldwide demand and supply of food, and how these factors are likely to interact, in order to develop a number of alternative scenarios. Key variables taken into account in these models include global population growth and, following from that, the total calories required, an estimate of dietary factors, and the potential for agricultural production based on the condition of the soil and other resources and on the productivity of plants and live-stock. The figures given below are derived from conservative esti-mates. In other words, this is not an alarmist picture of the global situation but a probable prognosis if the world sustains today's trends.

The most likely scenario, based on a number of more or less given factors, reveals that progress is generally being made and that by 2020 the outlook will have improved. But today's situation is not all that good. And, again, there is always the risk that ad-vances will blind us to the reality: the starting point for so many people is so far behind what is required for basic nutrition. Im-provements can be reinforced if a wholehearted effort is made to ensure that things become not just better but really good.

Supposedly More Calories, But . . .

Twenty years from now, as today, the world should, theoretically, be producing sufficient food for everyone to have enough to eat every day of the year. The average intake of calories will have in-creased to 2,902 per capita worldwide. Those who live in the industrialized parts of the world will by then have an average of 3,328 calories to work with, whereas people in the developing countries will have to make do with 2,806—but this amount is still adequate. Africa and South Asia, however, will still be plagued by shortages, Africa with an average of 2,276 calories per person per day and South Asia with 2,633—still too low. The number of people going hungry will have dropped only slightly, to an estimated 675 million, again with most of the undernourished concentrated in sub-Saharan Africa and South and Southeast Asia.

For children the overall picture will also be somewhat improved in 2020, with the number of undernourished children worldwide falling from the current 160 million to 135 million.9 But this masks the fact that the number of undernourished children in sub-Saharan Africa will increase during the same period. And in Africa the number of children whose growth is stunted (who are shorter than they should be, which indicates prolonged deprivation) will increase over the next five years: from 45 million to almost 50 million. In Asia, this number is expected to drop from about 125 million to 110 million. This is definitely a step in the right direction for Asia, but a modern-day Pontoppidan would still find material for many a tragic tale.

It is difficult to say whether the availability of micronutrients in the diet is likely to improve in the years to come, but if the figures continue to follow today's trends, then the situation will still be disastrous for a very large number of people.

But Aren't We Enjoying a Global Boom?

In attempting to envisage the world in 2020 we need models to refer to, for most of the factors involved are impossible to visualize. The United Nations estimated that the population of the world passed the six billion mark in November 1999. Working from that figure, we can estimate that the number of people on earth will increase by about 70 million every year for the next twenty years. This would give a global population in 2020 of approximately 7.5 billion, and even a slightly sharper upsurge in such major killers as malaria, pulmonary diseases, and AIDS is not likely to change this global figure by much, although in sub-Saharan Africa AIDS will temper population growth considerably. Nevertheless, the most reliable forecasts make it undeniably clear that, even in the most disease-ridden regions, populations will continue to grow in the developing countries.

The population in the industrialized countries is expected to increase by just under 4 percent from 1995 to 2020, reaching upward of 1.2 billion. The population of Africa is expected to reach approximately the same figure, an increase of 50 percent for the same period. India can expect a 36 percent increase and the developing countries as a whole, 40 percent. The pace of population growth is one of the decisive factors in calculating how much food will be needed in the various regions of the world twenty years from now.

The prediction is that we will be considerably better off by then—on average. The average annual income per person in the industrialized countries is expected to rise from 17,390 dollars (U.S. dollars) in 1995 to 28,256 dollars in 2020, calculating at 1995 price levels. The average annual income in developing countries will increase from 1,080 dollars in 1995 to 2,217 dollars two decades later, with the Latin American figure three times greater than the average. In Africa, the average annual income will still be as low as 359 dollars—just under a dollar a day—but even that is an increase over the 280 dollars a year on which Africans live today. The prospects for South Asia look somewhat brighter, with an increase in annual average income from 350 to 830 dollars.[10]

Food under Pressure on Many Fronts

The growing number of people will, in itself, lead to a need for increased production of crops, livestock, and fish. As poor people acquire greater buying power, their main demand will be for more food so that they can have enough to eat every day. Since the well-to-do are already eating as much as they want, the pressure on food production in industrialized countries will not increase by much.

The eating habits of the poor, such as the millions of people in the large countries of Asia, will undergo a change as they become better off: meals will become more varied, with less emphasis on staples such as rice. With more money in their pockets people tend to eat more meat and fish. The economic upturn will have a profound effect on food consumption. In the years leading up to 2020 a great many people will move from the countryside to the towns and cities of the developing countries, and this, too, will bring about a change in eating habits.

However, many calories are lost from the global food supply when people consume meat instead of food produced directly from plants, because farmers must first feed a great many calories to livestock in order to produce the meat. The "livestock revolution," now well under way, will markedly increase the demand for crops suitable for use as fodder, especially maize and wheat. Fortunately, poultry is the meat product that people want the most (an increase in demand of 85 percent is predicted)—fortunate because poultry convert plant calories to meat calories with a smaller energy loss than do cattle or pigs. Nevertheless, the demand for beef is expected to increase by 50 percent and that for pork products by 40 percent. This growing taste for meat will manifest itself primarily in the developing countries, where the consumption of meat will almost double. Even so, this means an increase of only 40 percent per person—to levels still only one-third of the amount of meat eaten by the average person in the industrialized world.

All in all, it is predicted that the world's farmers will need to harvest 40 percent more grain per year in 2020 than in 1995. Agriculture will also be under pressure to produce more root crops and other foods essential to developing countries. It looks like quite a job.

Hemmed in on All Sides

Historically, farmers in both the industrialized and the developing countries have been able to produce more food by applying better farming techniques, using improved plant varieties and livestock, and appropriating new land. This last ploy will not be of much help in the decades to come, however, unless we are willing to cause great damage to natural resources. Many places have no suitable untilled land left. In some regions the amount of farmland is restricted by the growth of towns, by road building, and by the increase in areas for recreational activities. Elsewhere farmers are being urged to plant forests and leave farmland fallow in order to provide more space for wildlife. And for many developing countries, limits on how much land may be cultivated are needed to prevent out-and-out environmental disasters. But regulations have little effect when desperate farmers can see no other way to earn a living and feed their families but to plow up more land. If we really want to protect the natural world and preserve the biodiversity of plant and animal life, we will have to coax better yields from existing fields. Sub-Saharan Africa and to some extent Latin America, with large areas of sparsely populated land, still have scope for plowing more land. But in other regions new farmland can be expected to make only a modest contribution toward the needed increase in productivity.

There is no getting around it: future demand for food calls for greater agricultural production. The figures calculated for 2020 presuppose that most of the increased volume of agricultural production will be provided by higher yields from fields in use today. For grain production, Africa could increase its output by 2.9 percent per year in the period leading up to 2020, with 1.2 percent of this deriving from the appropriation of new land. In the other regions, growth will be considerably lower—in the heavily populated countries of Asia, 1.5 percent, with the contribution from new land amounting to about 0.2 percent.

The predicted increase in the grain yield is not a foregone conclusion. In Africa, the gap between actual crop yields and the potential results of using more efficient techniques and more productive plant material is so great that any progress—any move toward providing more information and adopting better agricultural and economic policies—is bound to bring improvement. In Africa, where farmers cannot afford to invest in pesticides, herbicides, and fertilizers, the need for more productive plants, capable of with-standing the onslaught of pests and diseases and coping better with periods of drought, is overwhelming. Such varieties have not yet been perfected, but research is under way and these crops will be developed, as long as research funding continues and all the available approaches can be applied. This research investment is expected to provide healthy economic returns—as much as 40 percent per year. But the predicted growth begins from a very low starting point, an average yield of 1 ton per hectare. South Asia produces double this amount and by 2020 is expected to produce 2.5 tons per hectare. East Asia, however, shows yields of quite a different order: 4 tons per hectare currently, with a predicted increase to 5.5 tons in 2020.

In the more productive regions of the developing world, grain yields are not increasing at the same rate as before. In the early years of the Green Revolution, 1967–82, grain yields in the developing countries increased by almost 3 percent annually. During the period 1982–94 the annual rate of growth fell below 2 percent, and for the twenty-five years from 1995 to 2020 is expected to reach 1.5 percent. The hope of an upturn in global grain production, then, is based on the premise that investment in agricultural development and research does not decline and that reasonable price and market conditions prevail for farmers in the developing countries, which is where the main increase in grain yields must occur in the years to come. Sensible agricultural policies and a decent investment in agriculture cannot be taken for granted, if the situation in many developing countries over the last few years is anything to go by. So forecasts of an upturn may be too optimistic.

Where projections have been made for local areas, the situation in districts with a particularly pressing population problem is daunting. Because the groundwater level is falling, the chances of being able to use irrigation to the same extent in the years ahead are slim. The salting of plains from overwatering limits farming in certain areas, and the erosion of farmland causes a drop in yields or puts a stop to cultivation, particularly in very hilly country. Another serious problem is the depletion of soil nutrients in many areas, especially in Africa, where each farmer has so little land and so few resources that the soil is constantly under cultivation, with little fertilizer added to replace lost nutrients. Scientists call this "mining the soil." More of the vital nutrients—nitrogen, phosphorus, and potash—are depleted each year. And the farmer's fields yield less each year because plants are sapped of strength and fall prey to disease and insect attacks. It is a vicious circle, which can be broken only by better farming methods, improved plant material, and fertilizer.

Increased Production, but Uneven Distribution

Overall, the world's food supply seems to be holding up reasonably well right now. But regional differences require the transport of huge quantities of food from one place to another. Many countries both import and export grains in order to arrive at the right combination of grain for human consumption and for animal fodder. Typically, however, the developing countries must rely on increasing imports to cover the daily calorie requirements of their people, because they simply do not produce enough for everyone.

In order to meet the greater needs of developing countries in 2020, grain exports from the countries with a surplus will have to double. This sharp increase will have to be met by the United States, Australia, and the countries of the European Union and East Europe. Again, Africa, with its limited purchasing power, will have to take a back seat. Its imports are expected to increase from 10 million tons of grain a year in 1995 to almost 14 million in 2020, an increase of approximately 40 percent. In East Asia imports are expected to rise from 31 million to 71 million tons.

To meet the projected demand for more meat in the daily diet, meat imports to the developing countries will have to increase eightfold by 2020. This sounds like a lot, and such a mountain of food is hard to imagine, but it is still only a small share of the agricultural products that are being shuttled back and forth across national boundaries today. The world's total grain production now amounts to about 1.8 billion tons, and the models estimate that it will swell to approximately 2.5 billion tons by 2020. The grain that will have to be transferred to the developing countries to meet the demand in 2020 is estimated at 192 million tons, or more than 7.5 percent of the total global grain production—a jump of two percentage points over the current 5.5 percent.

The expected future movements of food between countries are obviously costly in terms of energy and foreign currency. Even today this transfer represents a massive supply operation. The main point—equally valid now and in the future—is that a major share of the food should be produced locally so that people with low purchasing power, most of whom live in rural areas, can earn more from agricultural production. We cannot rely solely on food being moved from region to region to make the global averages correspond to what will actually be needed for every single person in every corner of the globe.

Also, we must not overlook the crucial role of food production in rural districts as the main source of income not only for the farmers themselves but also for those who live in the surrounding communities. For this reason it is vital that agricultural productivity in the poorer countries be increased; we cannot be content with simply redistributing food and feed between rich and poor countries.

Things Are Not All That Great

A concerted effort to meet food needs in 2020 will require a marked improvement in agricultural production and a costly redistribution between countries with a surplus and those with a deficit. But the terribly disheartening aspect of what is, after all, an optimistic forecast is that our efforts will serve only to bring the numbers of the undernourished and malnourished down a little. Human suffering and want will still be a fact of life for millions of poor people. And the risk is always there that their daily lives will be rendered quite hopeless—their lives shattered by a deathblow—by rains that fail to come or insects that infest their maize crop.

This fear will continue to haunt countless farm families in Africa, Asia, and Latin America unless they are empowered to find appropriate solutions.

We have a moral obligation to mount a significantly more concerted effort that goes a good deal farther than the prospects presented by the statistical forecasts. To make the future decisively better for the poor of the developing countries, the only reasonable course is to take an objective look at all the options open to them and us. Those who live in the industrialized world have put behind them a desperate hand-to-mouth existence simply because it was a life too intolerable to lead or to contemplate. Shouldn't the poor of the developing world have the best possible chance to do the same?

4 · THE ALTERNATIVES

Global agriculture is frustratingly complex. Vast quantities of food are produced in high-yielding areas of the world. Surpluses pile up, and one could be forgiven for thinking there is more than enough food to go around. For many years, a number of industrialized countries have had record harvests; many developing countries, meanwhile, with declining yields or poor and erratic harvests, have had to supplement their food production with imports of grain and often with shipments of relief supplies. In some countries, crop production consumes a great many resources, through excessive use of manure and fertilizer and all too frequent sprayings with herbicides and insecticides. In others, irrigation systems are inefficient, drainage inadequate, and fertilizers unavailable. And in many areas new land is found for agriculture by appropriating woodlands and recultivating fallow land, thus destroying plant cover, wildlife, and biodiversity. Where farmers' plots are very small, the earth is often overcultivated to the point where the topsoil is eroded.

These are just some of the problems with global agriculture. In the industrialized countries, a consistent level of crop production is taken for granted. People who give any thought at all to agriculture are more concerned with health and environmental problems than with global food security.

Although the circumstances may be complex, the debate on the condition of the world is often one-sided, with isolated facts presented as "cure-alls" capable of addressing what the debaters see as the crux of the problem. In the debate on genetically modified foods certain arguments crop up again and again, decrying the need for any further development of genetic engineering.

Why Not Move the Grain Around?

For some people, one aspect of the global food situation has completely overshadowed all other arguments put together: enough food is now produced in the world to feed everyone. And, if the forecasts outlined in Chapter 3 are to be believed, everyone should be able, on average, to eat his or her fill every day. So why all the worry over production figures? Given that it is all just a matter of distribution, why not concentrate our efforts on doing something about that?

What is the likelihood that a massive redistribution exercise will do away with this particular aspect of the world's inequalities? There seems to be no great will to effect changes in global distribution in any form. Support for international development, for example, has in recent years constituted a dwindling slice of the gross national product (GNP) in most industrialized countries. Signs indicate that some of the public debt owed by the poorest countries to the richer countries will be written off, but it has taken a long time just to get that far. And goodwill is not exactly in evidence in the form of initiating long-term plans to help developing countries, along the lines of a food redistribution program, for example. In 1998 and 1999, donor contributions from the nations of the Organization for Economic Cooperation and Development (OECD) to the developing countries were slashed, because a great deal of money was needed to cope with the pressing problems in Kosovo. In effect, instead of the industrialized countries very slightly reducing their standard of living in order to increase their contributions, the well-deserved help to Kosovo was paid for by the poor countries.

Let's suppose, though, that a massive and prolonged effort was made to move food from areas with a surplus to areas with a deficit. Several problems immediately become evident. First, this redistribution could be accomplished only at the expense of long-term support programs aimed at fostering greater agricultural productivity in the developing countries. It would have to be funded through these programs because the people who need the food do not have the purchasing power to buy it. Second, the global surplus actually available is nowhere near large enough to make any real difference—unless, of course, we all become vegetarians. As we have seen, a fair amount of food is already being moved from one country to another. And third, in order to move massive quantities of food and feed from continent to continent and within each country, a vast transportation network would have to be designed and built, eating up many years' worth of investment dollars, not to mention the energy requirements and the damage to the environment.

Given these problems we cannot help feeling that the redistribution solution—that "the main problem . . . is not a question of productivity, but of distribution, right?"[1]—is simply too superficial. And, as we noted in the Introduction, developing countries certainly do *not* call this an answer. The distribution theory completely overlooks an important point: in almost all developing countries, even those where production is low, agriculture is the predominant industry and the most important source of income for the poor bar none. A large slice of the GNP is derived from agriculture, whether through production or processing, since agroindustry is often one of the few reasonably well established industries in poor countries. By far the largest share of jobs are related to agriculture. Seventy percent of the developing world's population lives in rural districts, and in many developing countries more than 50 percent of the people earn their living from farming. Agriculture is the trump card in the stakes for dynamic economic development in the developing world. It is not just the farmers and farm laborers who do well when agriculture is thriving. Local tradespeople and cottage industries also prosper, thanks to a multiplier effect that puts more money into circulation, in many places doubling the income made directly from farming.

Virtually every country that has managed to leave its low-income status behind has based its development on consolidated agriculture as the driving force behind the national economy. Countries such as South Korea, Taiwan, and Thailand, all of which are experiencing strong economic growth, are good examples, and China's successful economic development during the last twenty years also has its roots in a productive agricultural sector. There seems to be little chance that any country in the low-income bracket can skip this stage of development. In other words, we can find many good reasons why more food should be produced and why it should primarily be produced on small farms in low-income developing countries.

Let's Go Organic

In the course of using natural resources, agriculture can overuse or misuse them; resources can become worn out and perhaps permanently damaged. It is a worrying state of affairs, and many individuals and organizations around the world have focused their attention on solving these problems. They urge the adoption of alternatives to standard agricultural techniques in an attempt to reduce the wear and tear on the environment and redress the poisoning of soil and groundwater. This tremendously worthwhile endeavor has understandably won widespread backing, and agricultural research and development is striving to develop production techniques that will not harm the environment.

Consider the use of chemicals, for example. By the 1970s, the rapidly increasing and often excessive use of toxins in agriculture in both the developed and the developing countries provided some early warning signs of environmental damage. One result was a move toward production methods that forswore the use of chemicals of any kind, reverting to some extent to the farming methods of a bygone age, though still employing improved breeds of livestock and plant varieties and modern machinery. These methods are referred to as *nonchemical* or *organic farming*, because no chemical pesticides or inorganic fertilizer are used, only animal manure in raw or processed form or "green manure" from plants. Organic farming should not be confused with the so-called agroecological approaches, which focus on the use of available organic fertilizers and better cultivation methods but without the exclusion of chemical pesticides and fertilizers. Genetic modification can also be compatible with these approaches.

A farmer is required to adhere to a specific set of standards and methods in order to qualify as an accredited producer of organic foods, although the standards may vary among countries. Generally speaking, organic agriculture regards itself as the "natural" way, and GM crops have been deemed to have no place in the organic farmer's tool kit. All techniques, seed, and other inputs must meet the prevailing definition of "natural." Approved crop varieties developed by agricultural research other than genetic engineering, including tissue culture, marker-assisted breeding, and other modern biotechnology methods, qualify as natural.

For a number of reasons, though, organic farming does not necessarily result in nontoxic crops. If, for example, a plant is not protected from a disease or pest by spraying, the plant itself may compensate by producing its own protective substances, which will remain in the final product that goes to market. And not all natural plant substances are completely harmless, although usually we ingest them in such small amounts that they do not reach dangerous levels.[2] When pest infestations become too virulent, organic farmers have recourse to a "natural" weapon: spraying with a toxigenic bacterium, Bt (see Chapter 2). But while Bt may be a natural substance, it is still a toxin. Furthermore, some researchers have expressed concern about the effects of bacterial spores and of fungicides that can be used on organic produce.[3]

Organically grown produce may meet a need of consumers concerned about their health or the environment in a part of the world where people can afford to pay for what are necessarily more ex-

pensive foods. A problem arises, however, when the organic concept is propounded as a solution to the food problem in developing
countries. Farmers cannot achieve anywhere near the same levels
of productivity with purely organic methods as with modern farming methods, if all the land needed for green manure and livestock
manure is taken into account. Opinions vary on how great the drop
in productivity would be in industrialized countries if organic
farming methods were to become the norm. Pessimists say that
yields could fall by as much as half.[4] Initially, though, in certain
low-yielding regions of the developing world, this more intensive
and environmentally friendly farming would lead to a demonstra-
ble rise in production, although less so than if fertilizer and modern technology were used.

One strongly committed advocate of organic farming in developing countries cites a study of organic potato-growing in Bolivia.[5]
The yield on the traditional farms was 9.2 tons of potatoes per hectare; with the use of more labor-intensive organic methods this
was increased to 11.4 tons. Modern industrialized farms in the
same region produced 17.6 tons. The conclusion of the experiment
was that the economic gain per ton of potatoes—after the cost of
such items as fertilizer was deducted—was slightly higher for the
organic farmer than for the large-scale modern farmer and much
higher than for the conventional smallholder.

So organic farming looks pretty good, if one sees the environment as the cardinal issue. But for anyone who finds the developing world's food deficit—today's and tomorrow's—just as much
of a worry, the switch to organic farming is at best only part of the
answer, and only for specific areas. And we must note that the
comparison of the Bolivian potato yields in itself is not entirely
reasonable. If industrial fertilizer is replaced by organic material,
land will have to be set aside either for growing supplementary
plants to be used as green manure—in the Bolivian experiment lupines were used—or as acreage for livestock to produce manure.
This restricts the area available for growing potatoes, which in turn
makes for a smaller crop. When the cost of the additional land is

factored into the study, the figures for yield per hectare do not look so good. If we set aside the ecological risks of bringing more land under cultivation, organic farming may be a perfectly acceptable solution in regions with unused land that can be cultivated without damaging the environment. Such regions are becoming scarce.

Ethiopia has almost as many cattle as people.[6] The countryside attests to this fact; the vegetation on far too many stretches of land is chewed down to jagged stubble. Government authorities and researchers are trying to persuade farmers of the advantages of smaller herds of cattle. "If we seriously want to produce the volume [of manure] required to provide food for the whole world, global cattle production will have to be increased to between 5 and 6 billion head."[7] In other words, to produce enough manure to raise the same quantity of crops grown by modern methods, we would risk turning many countries into areas looking somewhat like parts of Ethiopia, with overcrowding and gnawed stubble on all sides.

As we have seen, green manure also requires space. In the Bolivian potato-growing example, 1.5 tons of lupines per hectare were used. In a Kenyan study, for every hectare of land used in maize production, 4 tons of weeds had to be lugged from hedgerows and roadsides to redress the loss of phosphorus and nitrogen.[8] This is considered women's work.

The organic viewpoint on nonorganic fertilizer is too restrictive to be generally applicable in developing countries. The organic approach may be ideal for restricting the spread of industrial fertilizer on overfertilized farmland in countries such as Japan, which consumes 200 kilograms of mineral fertilizer per hectare. In the Netherlands, on the other hand, it is not chemical fertilizers but the volume of cattle and pig manure that causes the leaching of nitrate into groundwater. But in Africa, the average amount of inorganic fertilizer used is only 12 kilograms per hectare.[9] And in many places on the African continent, the environmental challenge is, in fact, to achieve a balance in soil nutrients by administering a hefty dose of nitrogen-potash-phosphorus as often as the budget will allow, in order to prevent total exhaustion of the soil. While this may not comply with the orthodox organic approach, it has to be done. It is untenable to think that the loss of nutrients from farmland can be remedied in any other way in these regions.

When the amount of fertilizer applied is small, the nutrients are completely absorbed by the plants; nothing is left over to pollute the groundwater. In developing countries, smallholders tend to sprinkle the fertilizer precisely around the base of each individual plant, which ensures that it is absorbed; they simply do not have enough money to be extravagant with fertilizer. The finished product—the crop plant—is the same no matter whether green manure, cattle manure, or industrial fertilizer is applied.

Some proponents of organic farming assume that the labor-intensive nature of the farming is itself a good thing. And in some parts of the world—large areas of Africa, for example—this is a valid assumption. In other regions, including other parts of Africa, there are not enough hands to perform chores such as weeding even moderately well, which causes a bottleneck in the production process. As HIV/AIDS reduces the labor force, more and more areas of Africa will face labor shortages in agriculture. In Asia, where massive migration to the towns has raised concerns about the future of agriculture, farmers cannot be expected to work more hours to harvest each ton of grain. Asking people to spend even more time toiling in the fields is not the object of the exercise, particularly if they earn very little extra by doing so.

So the organic approach, while certainly a worthwhile option in regions with the space, the labor, and the consumer purchasing power to do things that way, is not a cure-all. Advice to developing countries to follow an organic model does not answer the problem of food security. And the assumption that the entire theoretical basis for modern organic farming as advanced in the industrialized world—including a rejection of the possibilities presented by chemical fertilizers and genetic modification—can meet the needs of developing countries and their realities borders on the paternalistic.

What's Wrong with the Status Quo?

For those who do not insist that the problem can be solved through redistribution or organic farming alone, but who would still rather steer clear of GM crops, the standard response is often a variation on the "business as usual" theme.

One of the "grand old men" of traditional plant breeding is the Nobel prize winner Norman Borlaug, now eighty-six years old and still actively involved in research. Borlaug was the chief architect of the high-yielding varieties of wheat, which broke the hunger barrier in the 1970s, a man who would have every reason in the world for sitting back, resting on his laurels, and consolidating a reputation founded on good, old-fashioned science. But Borlaug recognizes the limitations of his own findings: "There has been no great increase in the yield capacity of wheat and rice since the dwarf varieties sparked off the Green Revolution of the 1960s and 1970s. In order to meet mankind's rapidly escalating need for food, we need to come up with new and appropriate technological methods for increasing the yield capacity of grains."[10] And the statistics bear him out. As we saw in Chapter 3, the rate of growth of agricultural production has been declining over the past twenty years, and all the projections indicate that if we stick to the standard methods, this fall-off in growth rates will continue.

Perhaps so many people insist on maintaining the status quo, refusing to see any positive gains from genetic engineering, because the tried and true methods are familiar and seem perfectly natural. This is, of course, a somewhat dubious assumption when one considers that traditional plant breeding over the years has resorted to low-level radiation and chemical manipulation of plants in order to induce mutations, as well as various biotechnologies such as cloning, with the aim of developing better plant material.

Select any time point in the history of agriculture—say, agriculture and agricultural research in 1990—and we cannot really say that before this point things were still done in a natural way. Go back another ten or twenty years, and we still could not maintain that up to *that* point, plant breeders were doing no more than nature itself could have managed. Why, in the debate on natural versus unnatural, should we draw the line right here, right now, at the point where genetic engineering has entered the scene?

Long before humans intervened, nature overstepped its own species boundaries. Wheat researchers point to the crossing of grasses in the wild, which led, thousands of years ago, to the emergence of the first varieties of wheat: durum wheat can be traced back 5,500 years to the agricultural civilizations of the Middle East. Later, this development was taken a step further, when this wheat crossed with another variety of grass to produce the first bread wheat—"Nature's own genetically modified food," as Norman Borlaug describes it. And he reinforces his own assessment of the line between nature and human endeavor by stating that "the edible varieties of wheat which account for 98 percent of today's wheat varieties are genetically modified [by nature]."[11] This was the raw material he improved upon by crossbreeding wheat varieties held in gene banks, using traditional methods.

Why Not Just More of the Same?

The hefty increase in agricultural production over the past decade was partly due to the appropriation of new land. As we have already noted, possibilities for exploiting this option in the future are limited, and could be achieved only with negative consequences for the environment. Generally speaking, we cannot go much farther in that direction. In 1961, there were 0.44 hectares of farmland for every person in the world. Today the figure stands at 0.26, and the projections indicate that by 2050 it will fall to 0.15 hectares.[12]

Another vital factor for agricultural development in both industrialized and developing countries has been access to irrigation. As a rule of thumb, the yield on irrigated land is 2.5 times greater than on nonirrigated land. Irrigation systems have grown out of all proportion, with water flooded over fields—often quite indiscriminately—in every corner of the globe. In some areas this has caused massive damage to the environment; in Pakistan, for example, much of the former farmland is now saline.

Just as for land use, there is a limit to how much farther we can go with irrigation, given the increasing scarcity of fresh water, the competition for water from other industries, and a burgeoning urban society with a pattern of water consumption very different from that of rural villages. We can expect a greater insistence on saving water, as many drinking wells run dry outside the rainy season.[13] For example, the groundwater in countries such as Bangladesh has fallen drastically since the 1960s, in line with expansion of the irrigation systems. Africa, however, has a greater potential (but perhaps not the finances) for expanding its irrigation, since only about 5 percent of farmland is now irrigated. In Asia the figure is about 35 percent of the agricultural land.[14] Quite a bit can be done to make irrigation more efficient. Smaller amounts of water, closely geared to the plants' growing periods, can be applied. And irrigation systems should be better maintained to minimize leakage. But, again, irrigation cannot be expanded indefinitely.

The consumption of fertilizer and agrochemicals as an integral part of high-yield agriculture has increased dramatically. One reason for the success of the Green Revolution was that it was a package deal. Fertilizer enabled high-yielding plants to more fully exploit their yield potential, and agrochemicals restricted losses due to weeds, pests, and diseases. But in many places—again with Africa and parts of Asia as notable exceptions—the consumption of agricultural inputs has reached dangerously high levels. There is a logical limit to how much extra expenditure can be justified in return for only marginal gains in yield—quite apart from the strain on the environment.

As we have seen, traditional, efficient breeding of agricultural crops has worked very well in the battle against poverty and malnutrition, but the chances of making any dramatic progress in increasing yields are slim. With 80 percent of farmland in developing countries already planted with high-yielding varieties having some resistance to disease and pests, some concerns arise about the possibility of continued yield increases.¹⁵ On the other hand, the hope is that traditional breeding, backed up by and in combination with genetic modification, could break through the production barrier.

Careful, Progressive Change

We have not addressed here all the arguments for alternatives to GM crops, and we deal with a number of other arguments, pro and con, in the following chapters. But if one takes a long hard look at the future food situation in the poor developing countries, it is hard to see how single, easy solutions alone—no matter how alluring each may seem—can fill the bill.

As global solutions, the alternatives discussed in this chapter—as well as genetic engineering—have their limitations. None can be applied to all parts of the world, and some are simply unrealistic: they do not travel well, are not readily adaptable to the needs of certain communities, and do not meet the needs of more than a limited proportion of the world's poor.

If we were to conclude, though, that the solution must lie in more of the same, we would be overlooking environmentalists' solid arguments against pursuing our current line and the knowledge that, for any number of reasons, the old familiar technology cannot be expected to cope with the increase in production where it is most needed.

Advocates of the "carry on as we are" solution make the assumption that current products and methods of production are perfectly all right; they need no improvement. Sticking to what we know, just because it is familiar, does not show much initiative. In almost any gathering of international agricultural researchers, they all have tales to tell of improvements, small and large, on which they are working. Some of their discoveries could play a key role in making today's agricultural production better and more secure for consumers and farmers alike—for example, by banishing allergens from our everyday foods or rendering plants resistant to viral attacks. Some researchers employ genetic engineering because no other appropriate technology is available to them. If they are prevented from using these methods, they will also be prevented from arriving at solutions to the problems inherent in standard agricultural methods and in the foods we eat today. Unless we acknowledge that the situation is less than perfect, we will inevitably perpetuate a whole string of problems and risk pursuing the wrong course.

Drawing That Line Again

We are not, after all, strangers to genetic engineering. For a number of years now many of our medicines—including insulin, of enormous benefit to humankind—have been developed through the genetic engineering of bacteria and other microorganisms. And the food sector is not without its share of thus far uncontroversial GM products. Fermenting agents used in the manufacture of beer and cheese, for instance, were developed with the aid of genetic modification. These techniques often have advantages over traditional methods apart from financial considerations. For one thing, they avoid having to use natural animal products that may not be as pure as we might like—such as the rennet taken from calves' stomachs for making cheese (just as insulin was once obtainable only from animals).

And few people doubt the value of the advances in pharmaceuticals or ask their doctors whether the medicines prescribed for them have been produced with or without genetic modification. We are, for the most part, happy to be given the best treatment the pharmaceutical industry can provide. We see no powerful grassroots movement advocating a return to the pharmaceutical preparations of a bygone day. While many are concerned about the attempts by certain private corporations to extract exorbitant prices for pharmaceuticals, most people favor the research, development, and distribution of medicines needed to solve our health problems, even if they are developed by genetic engineering.

Before drawing the line between genetic modification for medicines and genetic modification for agricultural purposes, we should give careful thought to the beneficial aspects. In the industrialized world, the crucial issue is good health into old age; in other parts of the world it is adequate nutrition now and in the future. Ask a farmer in western Uganda whether she would prefer "natural" cassava or a GM variety that can combat leaf mosaic, a virulent plant disease. We can guess what her preference would be. But no one asks her. And some well-intentioned people in the industrialized world are inclined to believe she should not be asked. We argue that she should be given a real choice.

5 · CAN THE POOR BENEFIT FROM GENETICALLY MODIFIED FOODS?

Let's look at three short stories that illustrate the difference between the picture of genetic engineering that has been painted in the industrialized world and what researchers are actually doing.

- A top-ranking athlete is tested for performance-enhancing drugs after yet another victory, and the result is positive. The media milk this piece of news for all it's worth. Some weeks later, after a series of cross-checks and double-checks, it turns out a mistake was made. The athlete is completely exonerated, a fact that receives little attention in the press. Well, that's the way the cookie crumbles, some would say. But the athlete finds it hard to get his career back on track after being run through the media wringer.

- Great-grandmother's antique crystal glasses have been brought out for a family celebration. While washing the dishes, Dad almost drops one of the glasses on the floor. There are only eleven left as it is, so right then and there he is made to swear that he will never, ever break one of those precious glasses.

- It's a risky business being an electrician in Europe, where every wire carries a jolt of 220 volts. European electricians are trained in how to administer heart massage and mouth-to-mouth resuscitation just in case a worker accidentally comes in contact with a live wire. In the United States, where 110 volts is the norm, the risks are not quite so great, but the voltage is adequate to provide light and run most appliances. Doesn't it seem a bit bizarre for Europe to have opted for such a dangerous voltage?

We have here three rather silly anecdotes. Yet they serve to highlight some of the elements that GM crops are up against in the public debate. Here are a few examples that parallel these stories.

Several tired old chestnuts concerning the dangers of GM plants crop up again and again in the debate about genetic engineering. We have heard that a diet of GM potatoes killed rats in a laboratory in Scotland; that GM crops could kill harmless insects, even the beautiful monarch butterfly; and that GM soybeans carrying a gene from Brazil nuts contained a substance that could cause severe allergic reactions in consumers. As we have noted in earlier chapters, for all these stories either the results have been disproved by extensive research or the potential problem died a natural death during routine checking procedures. But one doesn't have to read too many letters to the editor or too many home pages on the Web to find that these stories are still doggedly making the rounds.[1] As the athlete in our first anecdote found out, retractions never have quite the same impact as hot news.

Many of our actions involve an element of risk, and not many things come with a lifetime guarantee—the only way a family can guarantee that no harm will come to its heirloom crystal is never to use it. Most forms of progress necessarily carry some risk. Of course, we weigh the risks and benefits and do everything we can to reduce the risks. And this is the understanding with which research on genetic modification is carried out, whether designed to solve medical, agricultural, or other problems. Refusing to embark on anything new until an official guarantee can be given that all the risks have been eliminated, as some parties would have it for GM plants,[2] is tantamount to bringing progress to a grinding halt. Such insistence on an ironclad lifetime guarantee ("our tests have confirmed that genetic modification will never, in any way, involve any element of risk whatsoever") runs counter to a simple, basic rule of science (and for that matter of life itself): it is impossible to prove a negative thesis. This assumes, of course, that we all agree that the debate surrounding a scientific subject should be conducted using arguments with a solid scientific foundation.

The system for supplying electricity in Europe treads the line between efficiency and risk. Making electric power completely safe is impossible, and attempts to do so would be hugely expensive, requiring massive restructuring of the national grids and a radical redesign of machinery and appliances. The resulting electricity bills would put a serious strain on the household budget. And potentially dangerous high-tension power lines would still be needed to distribute electricity to consumers. In the ongoing debate on GM plants, no evidence has been produced of any harm done. But many people do not even want the current switched on, no matter how many layers of insulation are wrapped around the cables.[3] Better to do without, they say.

Wanted: Some Dynamic Thinking at All Levels

Why is the debate on GM foods, pro and con, so heated? A major reason is that things seemed to happen so fast: GM plants entered the market so quickly and are already an irrefutable fact of life. (Another reason, a general distrust of new technology and of the competence and integrity of both government authorities and private companies, is discussed in Chapters 6 and 7.) While GM plants are having an enormous impact on certain crops and on the agricultural supply in some countries, in others they are seen as a threat. Genetically modified soybeans are the chief GM crop, accounting for 90 percent of all the soybeans sown in Argentina and 50 percent in the United States in 1999. Soybeans accounted for 54 percent of all GM crops under cultivation in the world in 1999, maize 28 percent, and rape and cotton 9 percent each.[4]

And why have GM crops become so widespread in such a short

time? These crops have fulfilled their promise. They provide robust yields with less work for the farmer and require smaller supplements of insecticides and pesticides that are friendlier to the environment than those used in traditional farming. All parties except the insecticide producers have profited: farmers, for whom the new crops mean lower costs or higher yields; consumer, because of less concern about pesticide residues; and manufacturers of seeds and herbicides, through larger sales and greater profits.

Looking at the specific qualities targeted in the first wave of GM plants, one might ask with good reason whether the new features made enough of a difference to the consumer to merit all the time and effort put into developing them. But then one could easily have asked the same question when the first ballpoint pens appeared on the market in the late 1940s. They were appallingly ugly, made of plastic in mottled tones of dishwater gray; they left ink stains on the pockets of men's white shirts; and they cost about one-and-a-half week's wages for, say, a delivery boy. As we know, though, both ballpoints and plastic were here to stay, improving in quality and dropping in price. Or think of people's first attempts to fly: weird contraptions were tried out with varying degrees of success on available patches of flat ground everywhere from the clover fields of Denmark to the prairies of North America. Sheer lunacy, respectable citizens were quick to agree. In comparison with these trial-and-error efforts, GM plants emerged as clear winners right from the start. The GM products already marketed have presented few problems, and those farmers who are looking for just what these plants have to offer get value for their money. Product development does not stop here, of course. Other crops, with fresh attributes and other combined benefits, will be forthcoming as quickly as laboratory experiments can be carried out, findings checked, and trials completed.

And herein lies the main obstacle to a constructive discussion of GM crops. Much creative, dynamic thought goes into discussion of the risks entailed in the new plant varieties. Granted, no ill effects have been proven, but it is not inconceivable that problems could arise. Or to put it another way, which reflects the arguments one hears so often, "Things may be going pretty well at the moment, but in the long run. . . ." All too rarely does the same dynamic come into play when looking at the beneficial effects: "There may not be much to shout about at the moment, but in the long run . . ." would be a reasonable parallel line of argument.

Having seen such a high degree of success with relatively new techniques in such a short time, we can fully expect a steady flow of results from this young branch of science as it develops in the coming years. This is particularly important for poor farmers and consumers in developing countries, who stand to gain very little from currently available genetic engineering technology. As the technology is developed, even more safeguards against ill effects will be incorporated—prompted, of course, by a healthy self-interest, since any evidence of serious errors or major problems would prove both expensive and disastrous for private and public investors in genetic modification. When the private corporation Aventis sold to farmers GM maize seed approved for livestock feed only, they failed to foresee that the GM maize (called StarLink) might end up in human food, for which it was not approved. According to informal sources, the cost to Aventis of this miscalculation, as of March 2001, has been in excess of a billion U.S. dollars, and the bills are still coming in.

Apparent Agreement on Many Points

At a conference on biotechnology and biosafety held by the World Bank in 1997 and attended by representatives of a number of U.N. organizations, research institutes, foreign aid systems, and developing countries, a short list was drawn up of some of the things that need to be done to make farming in the developing countries more productive. Most people would probably agree that this list goes at least some way toward covering the necessary agenda.

- Apply intensive farming techniques over a wider area, including, in some areas, increased fertilizer use.

- Conserve soil and water, with special priority to combating erosion.
- Maintain biodiversity.
- Improve pest control.
- Expand irrigation and make it more efficient.
- Improve livestock management.
- Develop new crop strains that are higher yielding, pest resistant, and drought tolerant.
- Reduce dependency on pesticides and herbicides.

The authors of this agenda, which won general endorsement at the conference, stated that genetic engineering seemed like a good means for fulfilling some of these goals: "At their best, the bioengineering techniques are highly compatible with the goals of sustainable agriculture, because they offer surgical precision in combating specific problems without disrupting other functional components in the agricultural system."[5]

There are no promises that genetic engineering will solve all ills, of course. From the days of the Wild West comes the myth of the cowboy hero's magical silver bullet, which never missed its mark and wiped out all the bad guys. In the debate surrounding genetic modification, few promise that this technology is a silver bullet. In fact, the disavowal of any such claims has become almost routine.[6] But not uncommonly, critics assume that such empty promises are being made.[7] Clearly, the debate is not well served by one side ascribing to its opponent patently unreasonable arguments to which all right-thinking individuals would take exception.

One of genetic modification's truly interested parties, a representative of one of the multinationals involved in seed production, who has a vested interest in profiting from this business, takes a sober view of what can be achieved. On the basis of the predicted population and its calorie requirements in 2025 and using figures provided by the FAO, he estimates that traditional plant breeding, increased use of fertilizer, and better irrigation systems could do 70 percent of the job; the other 30 percent will have to be fulfilled by various forms of biotechnology, including a good helping of genetic modification.[8] Thirty percent may not sound all that drastic, but it represents the extra calories that, for millions of families in the developing world, mean the difference between regularly going hungry and having enough to eat every day. And after 2025, agricultural production in the developing countries will have to go on increasing in order to cover the expected increases in the population.

Different Priorities

Even such a conservative goal as securing 30 percent of the growth in food supply over a twenty-five-year period through biotechnology may well prove difficult to attain. The private companies that are the major players in this field have not geared their research toward yield increases in developing countries but toward solving the problems of farmers in the wealthy countries. The explanation is very simple: this is where the money lies. So public research must do all it can to exploit the research potential of biotechnology to solve some of the high-priority problems in the developing world. Though the agendas of private and public research institutes differ, this does not mean that findings produced on one side cannot be absorbed or adapted by those working on the other. The substantial limitations and pitfalls of a constructive and close collaboration between private and public research are discussed in Chapter 6.

Research work can be classified in many different ways, depending on the interests involved: private versus public, industrialized world versus developing world, farmers versus consumers. These are not necessarily conflicting categories; a fair amount of overlap in potential benefits is possible for all those involved. But for simplicity's sake, we are considering here the research findings from a industrialized-world versus developing-world perspective, keeping in mind that to a large extent both sides have a common interest in furthering the development of robust high-quality agricultural plant material.

Big Hits in the Industrialized World

The first priority for agricultural biotechnology research in the industrialized world was to find a way to render crops resistant to the milder forms of weed-killer chemicals, so farmers could spray the weeds without damaging the crops. This accomplishment was environmentally sound because the milder forms of pesticides did little or no damage to the environment. This was a success with farmers, however, primarily because it eliminated tedious and time-consuming weeding close to plants and helped increase profit by cutting back on labor costs. It was also a smart way of turning a profit for the agro-industrial companies that sold the plant seeds, especially if they also happened to own the factories that manufactured the weed-killer chemicals. The breakthrough in this particular piece of research came about largely because the whole operation was technically feasible—the capacity for herbicide resistance being governed by a single gene.

The development of plants with a built-in pesticide (Bt; see Chapter 2) was another high research priority that proved achievable. It is popular with farmers in the industrialized countries because it cuts back on the costs of industrial pesticide and the labor for spraying it. It benefits consumers by reducing pesticide residues in food. By reducing frequent, copious spraying, it also benefits the environment. And it is as beneficial financially for the seed growers. The next logical research step, now under way, is to combine these two qualities in the same plant: resistance to pests and to weed killers.

Another front on which some progress has been made involves "shutting off" genes in crops—in fruit, for example, so that it ripens later and stands up better to transportation and storage, thus cutting back on waste. This could benefit farmers and wholesalers in the developing and industrialized countries.

More important from the consumers' point of view is the possibility of eliminating from crops both natural toxins and a predisposition to fungal infection, which would make the produce safer to eat. Research is also being carried out to reduce the allergenic effects of certain plants, such as wheat, peanuts, and soybeans. The allergenic tendencies of these plants cannot be effectively controlled through organic farming or bred out using conventional propagation methods.

The really big news in plant breeding today is the offensive now being mounted to improve the health-giving properties of plants. Vegetable oils containing a greater proportion of unsaturated fatty acids—better for human health—are in the offing. What better argument could there be for accepting GM foods than a vegetable oil marketed with the slogan, "Reduce your cholesterol with this oil." This type of advance is just around the corner. Another example is potatoes with a higher starch content—a real step forward nutritionally if they also happened to absorb less fat during cooking, so that people would be eating lower-fat French fries. Fruits could be developed to have a better aroma and greater sweetness, and no doubt more color could be added to the paler varieties—not directly health-giving properties, but perhaps encouraging consumers to eat more fruit.

Farmers are pleased to hear that in a few years seed producers will be able to offer them improved feed grains. Work is progressing nicely on development of a maize with kernels containing double the oil content of current varieties, increasing the oil from 3 or 4 percent to more than 6 percent. This means that farmers can give cattle, pigs, and poultry less feed concentrate, making them easier and cheaper to raise. And this will minimize the need to import feed grains, some of which come from the developing countries. This represents both a plus and a minus for the developing countries, of course: farmland now used to grow feed grains will be freed for growing human food, but exporting countries will lose revenue. Until recently, all attempts to increase the oil content of maize resulted in a drop in yield. Thanks to breeding work based on the mapping of the maize genes—not genetic modification as such, but a valuable spin-off from investment in new technology— this improvement can now be made without any loss in yield.

Other properties in grains will also be improved, among them increases in amino acids (giving us more and better protein in bread grain, for example) and micronutrients.[9]

Consumers and farmers are already reaping the benefits of the shift toward more environmentally friendly herbicides, and work is progressing on the development of plants capable of withstanding common plant diseases and insect attacks. This will lead to less use of pesticides and thus lower concentrations of agrochemical residue. Advances in this area could be of great help to farmers in developing countries.

Looking only at what private companies have in the pipeline, one would be hard put to see how current research provides any solution to the world's food supply problems. No significant effort has been made to raise the yield ceiling of the major crops, simply because the main objective of private industry is to win a share of the market in the industrialized world, where food is plentiful and relatively inexpensive. The failure of the real heavyweights in the field to invest resources in trying to break down the biological barriers to greatly increased yields is disappointing. This state of affairs has come under fire, and rightly so. Critics point out that promises made at the time of the first biotechnological breakthrough in the early 1980s have gone by the board in favor of lucrative—and easy—solutions to the profit-making agricultural concerns of the industrialized world. The first generation of results has left very few people convinced that the GM plants currently available are the solution to world food problems.[10]

Product Substitution: A Brief Interlude

When the inherent possibilities of genetic modification began to reach the public consciousness in the mid-1980s, one of the most troubling issues was product substitution: pictures of various plant products being replaced by factory-made flavorings concocted from who knew what microorganisms.[11] An obvious parallel was the ongoing transition from sugar to chemical sweeteners (not involving genetic modification).

Posing a risk for developing-country exports, a number of possibilities loomed on the horizon for replacing crops typically grown in developing countries, such as vanilla and cocoa, with manufactured substitutes, assisted by genetic modification. The massive production of starch, such as the root crop tapioca grown in Thailand, would be supplanted by efficient domestic production in countries that normally imported starch products. Or synthetic versions might be introduced, as has long been the case with rubber. But one could not be completely pessimistic about the prospect of replacing these products. The reliance of many developing countries on the sale of such commodities, with vast stretches of farmland devoted to plantations for export crops, was one of the main criticisms leveled at development policies. Critics insisted that developing countries should switch to domestic production of food to provide for their populations.

By the time genetic modification came along, the move toward substituting artificial flavorings for natural ones was already well under way; at the very most, genetic modification would speed up the process. Nor is this a straightforward developing-world versus developed-world issue; it is more a case of agriculture versus industry. The taste of citric acid in today's foods rarely stems from the lemons of southern Europe, and there are very few aromas that are not enhanced by ingredients produced in the laboratory. Sugar growing also suffers when substances such as "corn syrup" take over the job of sweetening our sodas and candy. We only need to look at food packaging to see how much things have changed. But a counteroffensive is now being mounted against substitute products: a growing demand from consumers in the wealthy countries for quality, flavor, and clear, comprehensible consumer information. So the market will most likely dictate the balance in this area, too.

The role of genetic modification in the development of substitute products has not been a decisive one. This is not an area in which the major biotechnology companies have invested a great deal, and we would have to go back to the early 1990s to find a time when the production of substitutes was a key issue in the debate on genetic modification.

The Priorities for Developing Countries

We can see the potential of genetic modification in quite a different light when we consider what is in the pipeline for developing countries. The list of GM crops for agriculture in the industrialized countries bears little resemblance to the range of plants cultivated in the developing world. Within the CGIAR group of research institutes (see Chapter 1), a small amount of biotechnology research (which involves much more than just genetic modification) is being carried out on maize, cassava, beans, rice, wheat, potatoes, sweet potatoes, barley, lentils, millet, sorghum, various fruits, and various multipurpose trees useful in agroforestry.[12] With the exception of maize, this list of crops is radically different from that of the private seed companies.

The list is dominated by the so-called orphan crops, those with very limited commercial appeal because they are grown mainly for personal consumption by poor smallholders. These farmers have very little money to spend on improved plant material, and certainly not every year—which is why the private sector has invested so little in research and development on these crops. Now, fortunately, national and international public research institutions are working on these plants.

A look at the research projects under way to improve rice, one of the main crops in developing countries and the world's most important grain, shows that the agenda of public sector research is squarely focused on the problems of small-scale farmers and poor consumers. The projects include work to develop resistance to viruses and other diseases, the ability to ward off attacks by pests, and the ability to tolerate flooding; and on the nutrition front, work to increase the iron content and add beta-carotene, which the human body converts to vitamin A.[13]

Researchers are hard at work mapping rice genes in order to come up with beneficial properties in a number of areas. Improving the plants' ability to withstand several plant diseases, especially various types of fungi, and to combat insects is high on the list of priorities. The possibility of earlier flowering and hence a shorter growing season is also being explored, and work is being done to improve the capacity of rice plants to tolerate drought and cold. A considerable slice of the research on rice is funded by the Rockefeller Foundation. Since the late 1980s, the Rockefeller Foundation has invested about a hundred million U.S. dollars in research collaborations and the training of researchers in developing countries. It has also donated smaller amounts for research in the two leading countries with special knowledge of rice, Japan and South Korea.[14]

Another promising genetic modification project involves research to make crops more tolerant to salt, so they can be watered with brackish water, survive minor flooding in coastal regions, and, perhaps most important, grow on soil that has a higher than normal salt content following years of irrigation. This would allow a return to farming on large areas such as the plains of Pakistan that have been rendered infertile by salt deposits left by years of indiscriminate irrigation during the overzealous early stages of the Green Revolution. There are some signs that success in this area would also lead to plants that make more efficient use of water and could therefore be grown more successfully in areas with low or unreliable rainfall, as in large parts of southern Africa, North Africa, and the Middle East.[15]

As mentioned earlier, great strides have been made through traditional plant breeding to endow grains and other crops with higher vitamin and mineral contents, but adding vitamin A to rice became possible only with the advent of genetic modification. Further development of these techniques could also help concentrate micronutrients in those parts of the plant typically eaten by human beings—the kernel or the root, say—and make possible the neutralization of plants' so-called inhibitors, which limit the ability of humans to absorb nutrients. With the newly developed rice plants, 30 to 50 percent of an adult's daily iron requirement could be covered by a bowlful of rice.[16]

Food enrichment of this kind is clearly a boon to poor consumers, but this very factor may define its limitations. In a market that lacks the money to pay more for better quality, farmers would have no great incentive to abandon their traditional varieties for this reason alone. The higher content of micronutrients, however, may also boost plant growth. If the plants are more vigorous and better equipped to ward off disease, then it is in farmers' interest to switch to the new varieties. Again, this seems to be a win-win situation: better for farmers and better for consumers. This research to improve the micronutrient content of crops was initiated in the mid-1990s. While the aims of the research were promising, the means of attaining them were unclear. Since then we have seen the development of the new "golden rice," funded through the Rockefeller program and using genetic engineering techniques.[17] (The rice is golden because beta-carotene lends the plant a carroty-orange tinge.) The tempo of work and the confidence in the imminent practical application of the golden rice are building up fast, inspiring renewed determination to find more ways to increase the micronutrient contents of staple foods.

In Kenya, prolonged efforts to render sweet potatoes resistant to viral attacks yielded no useful results until the advent of genetic engineering. A simple technique performed during propagation, a tissue culture that some farmers can carry out themselves, ensures healthy cuttings from the new, viral-resistant variety, which is expected to reach the market by 2002. Further work is also being done to make the new variety resistant to a particular beetle, another of its enemies. This doubly strong variety should be ready by 2004. In a really bad year, viral attacks alone can reduce the sweet potato crop by as much as 80 percent, and losses are seldom less than 20 percent when the virus is rife in the fields.[18]

Organically minded rice farmers in Asia will be happy to hear that Japanese researchers have made good progress with the development of GM varieties that boost the effect of a natural method of pest control, a biopesticide known as NPV. Spraying can be reduced considerably because the leaves of this new variety require only 3 percent of the normal dosage of NPV to resist pests.[19]

Other examples of the application of genetic modification have been mentioned in earlier chapters, including work on developing grains that can capture nitrogen from the air, thus doing away with or reducing the need to add nitrogen fertilizer. And we could go on cataloguing the bright prospects in the researchers' work plans, among them such truly grand visions as improved exploitation of sunlight during the growing process or the potential for GM grains to thrive in tracts of land containing high natural levels of aluminum—barren plains or stretches of savannah that cannot otherwise be farmed.

China has made a massive investment in GM cotton and a number of GM food crops including rice, potatoes, tomatoes, and maize. The aim is to ease the strain put on the environment by irrigation and agrochemical toxins and to achieve a badly needed increase in plant yields. Although the Chinese are not saying much about it, they have obviously channeled much of their research capacity into genetic modification programs. The spiraling double helix of the DNA molecule appears in sculptural form in squares and marketplaces and is carried high in the parades on national holidays.[20] The whole undertaking has been publicly financed, apparently riding on a wave of official enthusiasm. China was one of the countries invited to take part in an extensive publicly funded project to map the human genome. Involvement in such an undertaking calls for greatness in every sense of the word. In other countries, the debate on GM crops may continue to go round in circles or things may eventually grind to a halt, but China appears to be moving full-steam ahead.

Who Reaps the Benefits of All This Potential?

Although focusing genetic engineering on developing-country crops offers many possibilities for boosting agriculture, the benefits will not necessarily be reaped by the poor, whether farmers or consumers. To target the benefits to these groups, a concerted effort will have to be made. Improving crops that are grown predominantly by smallholders for their own consumption or are bought by the very poor is a good place to start. A number of the crops already mentioned fit into this category. We discuss here the cultivation of sweet potatoes in Kenya and potatoes in Mexico.

In Kenya, a careful analysis was made of the likely impact of the improved varieties of sweet potatoes.[21] These tubers are typically a poor person's fare, more often than not grown by women. Most are eaten by the smallholder families themselves and the rest sold at the local market or in the poorest quarter of the town. The GM variety with a combined resistance to both virus and beetles is expected to increase yield by 43 percent, reducing the growing costs per hectare by 36 percent. Because Africa's farmers never put all their eggs in one basket, biodiversity in agriculture is high; the new plants will replace only some varieties, possibly only 50 percent. In order to comply with farmers' and consumers' desire for variety, researchers are working on the genetic modification of five different types of sweet potato. According to the calculations, however, even this limited shift toward the new varieties will result in an annual gain of more than twelve million U.S. dollars—and sweet potatoes are grown on only 2 percent of the farmland in Kenya.

Economists can now produce all sorts of information from their models, so we can calculate that three-quarters of the gain from GM sweet potatoes will go to farmers, the remainder to consumers in the form of lower prices. The calculation is a relatively simple one, for several reasons: sweet potatoes are neither imported nor exported, researchers are close to perfecting the finished product, and they know the farmers' feelings about the new varieties from trials in the test fields. Some of the technology used in the research has been donated by the U.S. company Monsanto, which has entered into various collaborative agreements with public research organizations. Monsanto has agreed to give free access to a limited amount of technology to countries where it cannot make money from its research. Even allowing for a certain number of hidden costs in the supposedly free element of the operation, investing in improved plants makes good business sense for a country like Kenya, since the annual return is estimated at 60 percent of the research and development costs invested. This figure, however, masks Kenya's costs in defraying a fair amount of the general initial expenditure on the new technology, sweet potatoes being the first GM crop to be test-grown in the country.

Another example, from Mexico, is slightly more complicated, inasmuch as it deals with potatoes grown by both small- and large-scale farmers and sold to people at all income levels.[22] Moreover, industry and various consumer groups favor different potato varieties, making any predictions of the impact of this GM crop on different categories of farmers and consumers somewhat more difficult.

In Mexico, the cost of producing a ton of potatoes is almost the same for farms of all sizes, but yields can vary widely, from 11 to 31 tons per hectare. The big farms produce 64 percent of the potato harvest, the medium-sized farms 24 percent, and the small farms just 12 percent. What these figures do not tell us is that, although the cost may be the same for all, the small-scale farmer has an outlay per hectare of approximately fourteen hundred U.S. dollars, while the big growers are investing almost three times as much because they spray liberally with agrochemicals and purchase new, healthy seed potatoes at regular intervals. The small-scale farmers rarely use agrochemicals—only when things really get out of hand—and instead of buying seed potatoes, they set aside potatoes for seed or swap with their neighbors, thus saddling their crops with inbred diseases that are perpetuated in the seed potatoes. They lose up to 35 percent of their crop to viral diseases, while the medium-sized farms lose 25 percent and large farms 15 percent to these diseases.

Mexican potatoes are prone to three serious types of viral infection. Monsanto has granted Mexico some free use of technology to promote virus resistance, with public international institutions acting as intermediaries. But there is a twist to this tale. The small-

and medium-scale farmers favor a reddish-skinned potato that has a reasonable level of resistance but is bought only by the poor. Large farms produce white potatoes for sale to well-to-do consumers and to industry, but these are also grown and sold in the United States, Monsanto's home market. In just a few years' time, when the North American Free Trade Agreement (NAFTA) comes into full play, the larger Mexican farmers will have a good chance of competing with U.S. farmers. Herein lies the twist: the technology agreement with Monsanto permits two of the antiviral genes to be introduced into all varieties, but the third antiviral gene will be used—free of charge—to improve only the red varieties favored by poor consumers and small farmers. For small farms this would seem to be a good deal. They can produce many more potatoes per hectare and cut costs considerably. With the new varieties they get approximately three times more out of each hectare than do the large farms, in terms of improved yield or reduced expenditure. Once again, the middle-sized farms fall somewhere in between. Small-scale farmers stand to gain the most because they no longer suffer the heavy losses caused by the virus. The large farmers benefit only slightly, since they are already protecting themselves against the virus the costly way, by spraying. And they still have to expend a certain amount on spraying against the third and most dangerous virus that infects the white potatoes—either that, or buy the fully improved varieties, which are sure to become available commercially.

These bright prospects may not be fully realized, however. The small-scale farmers are not in the habit of buying new seed potatoes. An analysis of the probable state of affairs should farmers simply carry on as they are indicates that both the medium- and large-scale farmers would rapidly switch to the new varieties, but small farmers would probably be slow to do so, and then only to a limited extent, say 30 percent of the farmers.

A campaign to distribute the new potatoes through a publicly funded program exchanging "old potatoes for new," as has been done with other crops in a number of developing countries, would undoubtedly see small farmers lining up to get their hands on the improved varieties. Within a few years they would go over to them completely. And from then on they could set aside a little of their own harvest for seed. This is an illustration of the importance of policies to help ensure that modern technology is benefiting the poor.

It Could Not Be Simpler

At their most pessimistic, agricultural researchers are filled with misgivings for the future, especially for Africa, where farmers are working with technology and farming methods that produce very low yields. When feeling more optimistic, researchers take pleasure in the many ways in which successful, simple, and suitably tailored research findings have improved the daily lives of small farmers in many parts of the world—including Africa.

Genetic modification of agricultural crops deserves to be viewed in an optimistic light, and the examples cited in this chapter illustrate why this is so: a single element, a new plant, is introduced into existing agricultural production with a minimum of fuss and maximum impact, and without other changes in the production system. Researchers and government authorities may have found it hard going to get this far, but to the farmers it seems wonderfully simple.

"It's All in the Seed!"—That's the Good News

When there is good news to tell, no agricultural consultant worth his or her salt would miss out on the opportunity to give away a couple of trade secrets. The "miracles" produced by the new varieties of plants bred by traditional methods resulted as much from the greater degree of care the plants received as from their high-yield pedigrees—care such as thorough weeding, the use of compost to improve the soil, and special efforts to combat wastage and loss after harvesting.

All the data we have quoted on the benefits to be gained from the newly developed GM crops are based solely on what the improved plant material itself is capable of yielding. The reality could be very different: either worse, because people think the new plants can do it all themselves, or (more likely, based on past experience) better, because people think a little extra work at the start of a new enterprise is worth the trouble, especially an enterprise that promises them greater profits and more food security.

6 • WHO SETS THE AGENDA?

In this chapter we look at the various parties that influence decisions on whether genetic engineering in agriculture is allowed to develop and under what conditions. Consumers, companies, lobbyists, advocacy groups, politicians, the news media, and farmers—all are part of the debate. A first question, of particular importance to this book, is who sets the agenda for poor people and poor countries? Next is the knotty problem of ethics: are we venturing into forbidden territory, and what is the potential for harm or good? And finally, who owns the technology, and is there a move toward monopoly?

Positions for or against the use of genetic engineering in food and agriculture in the industrialized countries are frequently extrapolated directly to the developing countries. If Europe, North America, and Japan do not want this technology, wouldn't it be inappropriate to promote it for developing countries? Not necessarily. Food and agricultural problems differ widely between poor and rich countries, so the most appropriate solutions might also differ. We mention here just a few reasons why a position against the use of genetic modification in food and agriculture in industrialized countries might be perfectly compatible with its promotion in developing countries.

Poor people in the developing countries spend 50 to 80 percent of their incomes on food, compared with the 10 to 15 percent spent by people in the European Union and North America. Technological advances in agriculture that could result in lower production costs and cheaper food would be extremely beneficial to low-income consumers. Productivity gains in industrialized-world agriculture are much less likely to result in consumer gains, for three reasons. First, price changes for items that command only a small share of the family budget are of little concern to consumers. Second, only a small part of what consumers pay for at the grocery store in industrialized countries comes from the farm; packaging, transportation, storage, and advertising are a big part of the price. Not so for low-income consumers in developing countries. And third, existing agricultural policies in the European Union and North America tend to reduce the extent to which productivity gains in farming are passed on to consumers.

With 50 to 80 percent of the population living in rural areas, poor countries are much more likely to be interested in productivity increases in agriculture than are rich countries, where only 2 to 5 percent of the population depends on agriculture for its income. Many low-income countries are currently at a stage of development where agriculture is the only viable lead sector for broad-based economic growth. They are clearly much more interested than are rich countries in ways of increasing productivity in agriculture.

If each country were to make its own decision on the use of genetic engineering technology based on its perceived benefits and risks, there would be no problem. But rich countries and groups of well-fed individuals sometimes try to impose their views on developing countries and poor people who are constantly fighting for their daily bread. This interference is not welcomed by those responsible for food and agriculture in the developing countries. Consider some recent comments from spokespersons for the developing countries.

In a recent article in the *Washington Post*, the Nigerian Minister of Agriculture, Mr. Hassan Adamu, stated, "We do not want to be denied this technology [agricultural biotechnology] because of a misguided notion that we do not understand the dangers or the future consequences. We understand . . . We will proceed carefully and thoughtfully, but we want to have the opportunity to save the lives of millions of people and change the course of history in many nations. That is our right, and we should not be denied by those with the mistaken idea that they know best how everyone should live or that they have the right to impose their values on us. The harsh reality is that, without the help of agricultural biotechnology, many will not live."[1] We might expect a similar statement from a European or American minister of health if groups from African countries were instigating opposition in Europe or the United States to the use of modern biotechnology to develop a cure for cancer.

Professor Jennifer Thomson of the University of Cape Town, South Africa, puts it this way: "Rich countries may engage in lengthy disputes about real or imagined risks. We suggest that is largely a luxury debate. From the perspectives of many developing and newly industrialized countries, agricultural biotechnology's benefits are very real and urgently needed today and indispensable tomorrow. The developing world cannot afford to let Europe's homemade problems negatively impact the future growth in our countries."[2] The African Biotechnology Stakeholders' Forum also expresses concern about "mounting attempts to curb the evolution and development of biotechnology in Africa" and "that those in the industrialized countries continue to assume they know what is best for Kenya and the rest of Africa."[3]

P. Chengal Reddy, president of the Federation of Farmers' Associations in Andhra Pradesh, India, expresses great concern about the failure of "certain well-known activist organizations in developed countries" to take into account the opportunities that modern agricultural technology offers to improve the well-being of the poor in Asia. He suggests that we should "leave the choice of selecting modern agricultural technologies to the wisdom of Indian farmers."[4]

Another reason why the perspectives on modern biotechnology may differ between rich and poor countries is the difference in the relative importance of various health problems. Cancers, diabetes, heart diseases, and obesity are the overriding health problems in many industrialized countries, while child malnutrition and lack of access to enough food may be the most critical health problems facing poor people in developing countries. Clearly, the most appropriate solutions vary with the problems that need to be addressed. The willingness to take risks is likely to differ between those who are well fed and those who are fighting for their subsistence. Poor and rich should each make their own benefit-cost calculations. Imposing the views of the rich on the poor may result in misguided policies and action.

The agenda should be set by those who have to live with the consequences of the resulting action, not by some misguided belief that people in rich countries know what is best for the poor countries and poor people of the developing world.

The Battle for Souls

Anyone who tries to keep abreast of reports on GM crops issued by various environmental organizations around the world will soon get the impression that genetic modification is a dirty and dangerous business, and that one should avoid it like the plague while at the same time actively opposing it.

Among all the invective against GM foods, one term in particular—"Frankenfood"—has stuck. Plenty of well-organized photo opportunities are arranged for the press, featuring demonstrators clad in protective clothing making commando raids on test fields, primarily in the United Kingdom (whether planted with GM crops or not). On Greenpeace Denmark's Web site, in the section on genetic modification, a half-grown human embryo floats inside the amniotic sac of a transparent red tomato. "Does this picture scare you?" the text asks. Then it goes on to allay our fears slightly: "Don't worry! It's not a reality—yet."[5] Further down the page one has the option to click on <Information on genetic modification>, although this might not be the best place to look for any balanced, unbiased information on the subject. Altogether, by any reasonable standard, this is an outrageous piece of newsmongering.

Nevertheless, this kind of message has the desired effect, and, consciously or not, the mainstream press tends to reinforce it. In January 2000 a leading Danish newspaper, *Politiken*, presented a fairly low-key report—which nonetheless took up seven columns on the front page of its Sunday edition—on "the hunt for GM food,"[6] reporting demands by retailers that their suppliers be up-front with them about GM products. Buried somewhere in the middle of the report are these words of wisdom on the GM ingredients (in this case maize and soybeans) of foods: "scientists say that they are neither more nor less healthy than traditional maize and soya products." Less than a week later, one of *Politiken*'s business journalists dissociated himself from this opinion, under the headline: "Healthy Pigs Could Prove Costly."[7] The gist of his article was that Danish pork producers were just beginning to realize the expense of producing a pig for export to Britain that they could guarantee had at no time been fed GM fodder. That a diet free of GM fodder would render a pig especially healthy is not backed up by any evidence, but biotechnology might not be this particular journalist's forte. On three occasions in eighteen lines he refers to these pigs as "gene-free . . . from the first link in the chain to the last." A very lightweight pig, one could say. Setting aside these rather humorous claims, is it too much to expect the press to investigate why the words "neither more nor less healthy" don't hit home, even among their own ranks? The headline (and the gist) of the business journalist's story could just as easily have been, "Would You Believe It? Britons Want to Pay More to Get the Same!" But in cases like this, the press knows what makes news.

In a leading article in January 2001, the British newspaper *The Independent* presented a different perspective: "Monsanto has done more to damage public confidence in biotechnology than even the most alarmist press reporting of the 'Frankenstein foods.' British confidence in biotechnology—once seen as the next 'white hot' hope of the technological revolution—can be restored, but it will require a conscious effort by the scientific community and by governments to return to the idealistic ambitions which guided the early phases of research."[8]

The Customer Is Always Right

According to some of these anti–GM food tirades, it seems to be an established fact that GM foods constitute some sort of time bomb. Consumers—that is to say, voters, the people who read the newspapers or watch television news—obviously take exception to all the sinister goings-on in biotechnology. While the majority of news reporting is objective, some parts of the news media have helped demonize genetic modification, often leading the opposition to GM foods more or less uncritically. Other parts of the media, notably many of the larger U.S. newspapers and public radio and television, are trying to provide more factual information to enlighten the public debate. In an editorial in February 2001, the *Wall Street Journal* makes a plea that probably reflects the views of many U.S. newspapers: "Will someone please explain to us just what, exactly, is wrong with genetically modified foods?"[9]

One problem in the discussion about genetic modification seems to be a lack of understanding—a poor grasp of biology. Only 45 percent of Americans questioned in a trans-Atlantic survey could give the correct answer to the following question: "Do ordinary tomatoes contain genes, or is it only genetically modified tomatoes that do so?"[10] And the Americans are not alone. Only 20 percent of Greek and 50 percent of Dutch subjects answered correctly. Seniors might be excused for not knowing that every living thing is made up of genes, because genes weren't discussed much when they were in school. The steady flow of misinformation dispensed by the press has not done much to redress that situation. Again, is it too much to expect the media to act as a source of reliable information, to help their readers understand the matters under debate?

This is the starting point for some of the problem. Ignorance of the basic facts provides the perfect climate for influencing public opinion—if necessary through misinformation, fear-mongering, and ill-founded conclusions. Added to this, sadly, are the all too frequent true horror stories of unhealthy products and poor hygiene in the food industry unrelated to biotechnology.

In many countries, skeptical consumers are in the majority. A survey carried out in 1995 found that in Sweden, 65 percent of the population believed GM foods could involve serious health risks. In the United Kingdom, the figure was 39 percent. In the United States, however, it was only 21 percent.[11] (This substantial difference between Europe and the United States is a story in itself.) Not many of those who decry genetic modification can cite informed scientific sources on the subject, because "neither more nor less healthy" reflects the general thinking in scientific circles. And, as we saw in Chapter 2, some scientists maintain that the safety measures governing GM foods are tighter and more likely to find potential problems than those for conventional foods.

As the manufacturers and supermarket chains know, the customer—the consumer pushing the shopping cart—is always right. As soon as the first ripples of panic struck the retail trade, everyone from Nestlé's baby foods to British and continental European supermarkets, including the full gamut of British food giants, warned against foods containing GM ingredients. Consumer organizations spoke out: either consumers should completely avoid such products or, more reasonably, they should demand to be informed about exactly what their foods contain—because manufacturers might try to avoid full disclosure.[12] Japanese breweries, for example, have guaranteed that their beer is not made from GM grain. It is doubtful, however, whether they will see fit to inform beer drinkers that the beer probably derives its taste from GM brewer's yeast.

The latest triumph for the anti–GM food groups has come with the swift about-face in the production of dog food by the French giant Royal Canin.[13] Since the close of 1999, the company has declared its three European factories off-limits to any and all GM ingredients, and a phase-out is already under way in Argentina, Brazil, and the United States. So now Fido can rest easy—no bioengineers are tampering with his food.

Greenpeace has appointed itself to speak for the cause, for "the [E.U.] peoples' demand for a strong line on GMOs [genetically modified organisms]."[14]

Politicians Jump on the Bandwagon

The power of the anti–GM food lobby is partly the fault of governments. In democratic politics today, the first thing one learns is how to count the number of seats in parliament or congress and calculate what is needed for a majority. Next comes the ability to interpret opinion polls, and to respond in such a way as to improve one's standing in these polls.

It wasn't always this way. In the 1980s a broad political consensus was reached in many European countries on the introduction of excellent and far-sighted legislation to prepare Europe for the advent of biotechnology, which was soon to make substantial inroads into people's daily lives. This did have some adverse repercussions, especially over the new prospects for medical treatment, but common sense prevailed and the situation was defused by sensible legislation, grounded in a clear awareness of the obvious benefits to be derived from using the most advanced technology available to safeguard the health of citizens. The matter gave rise to a lively and heated public debate and the painting of some apocalyptic scenarios, but there was no witch-hunt. Inevitably, the most heated arguments concerned the definition of life, fetal diagnostics, organ transplantation, and other such difficult matters. These questions were dealt with in both personal and political terms through fruitful and often bold dialogue. Both the lack of bias and the scientific ballast did wonders for the credibility of the debate.

When GM foods appeared on the scene, all hell broke loose. Things started quietly enough with laws passed in various countries, additions to the joint E.U. legislation, and rules for dealing with the new technology and its products. Security measures, authorization procedures, and the establishment of decision-making bodies were all worked out. Ideally, public research had to keep up more or less with the pace set by the private laboratories, so national bodies were set up to evaluate and deliberate on the numerous questions that arose. The whole idea was to have a well-ordered program governed by rational arguments.

The issue never had much political cachet, however; politically speaking, the matter was more or less left out in the cold. European industry and agriculture were gearing up to enjoy the benefits of the new technological breakthrough. Some intriguing alliances were formed in order to operate in specific areas. Because it takes time to arrive at a crop that is ready to be tried out in test fields, not much was yet heard from the laboratories and greenhouses. And not the slightest response was heard from the media. Then some environmental organizations began to take notice, and they apparently came to the conclusion that GM plants were the next potential ecological and social disaster.

In the United States plant biotechnology had progressed quite a bit farther. By the mid-1990s, the new GM varieties of soybeans were due to arrive in Europe. And this was entirely legal, according to the rules and procedures laid down under the European system. In 1997, a cargo of animal fodder was scheduled for arrival in a Danish port. As before and since in a number of other European harbors, the importer found himself in the middle of a maelstrom. Before he could bring the cargo ashore, a media blitz was ensured: protesters, banners, cordoned-off areas, a large police presence. This particular cargo of grain just happened to be selected for an act of civil disobedience, as its advocates called it, a symbolic event; the feeling that someone should do something about the GM food question was fairly widespread. Later that same year there was another outcry in Denmark. Rumor had it that another boatload of GM fodder was headed for a Danish port: GM maize, which had begun to sprout while in transit, which for some reason seemed to add to the sense of impending disaster. A cry went up for the authorities—assumed to be failing in their duty as watchdogs—to nip the perceived scandal in the bud without delay. The press followed every move. As things turned out, the control systems functioned properly and everything was done by the book. This did not make headlines in quite the same way as a potential scandal, of course.

With the continuing advances in technology, an updating of the European rules for the testing and cultivation of GM plants was called for. By 1999 this had become a rather touchy issue. The major exporting countries with lots of GM seed to sell—the United States in particular (the European Union being a vast agricultural market for American farmers)—were pressuring Europe to make a decision. But the European politicians were not to be hurried, even though the outlines of an updated compromise document to replace the 1990 directive were gradually beginning to take shape. Then, in the summer of 1999, the results of the first monarch butterfly experiment in the United States (see Chapter 2) hit the headlines, and European ministers for the environment promptly backed off. This was now an unpopular case to legislate. The butterflies became the surprise exhibit, proving that too little was known about the possible effects of genetic modification. All fifteen countries of the European Union temporarily stopped issuing permits for the cultivation of new GM crops; talks on a new directive were put on the back burner. By late fall, further experiments with the monarch caterpillars had proven the entire matter was a false alarm, but not one European minister for the environment took the opportunity to get the ball rolling again. In other words, the politicians allowed themselves to be driven into a corner, and it is unlikely that any initiative will be forthcoming from that direction. With some important exceptions, notably the United Kingdom, the European political establishment seems to be firmly in the anti–GM food camp.

In the United States the situation is very different. The U.S. government is firmly in support of the development and commercialization of GM seed and food, subject, of course, to what the government agencies—the Environmental Protection Agency, the

Food and Drug Administration, and the Department of Agriculture—consider appropriate testing and approval. Where rules are violated, the government response is swift and decisive, as shown by the StarLink case discussed in Chapter 5. But such incidents are dealt with on the perceived merit of the case rather than as a general opposition to GM food, such as is found in some European governments.

Big Business Pulls Back

When the big seed-producing companies started to pool all available research to produce effective GM seeds for the farmers of the industrialized world, they appeared to be sitting on a goldmine. Granted, major capital investment and a great deal of expertise would be called for to arrive at high-quality products: the development phase was long, the technology expensive, and the authorization procedures rigorous. But this looked like such a good business proposition that in the 1980s and 1990s, the chemical industry giants began to buy up the big seed producers in a series of international deals. The buyers saw this as a way of getting in on the new developments. By tailoring their weed killers to the needs of a particular seed, they would have an automatic market every time that seed was sold.

Mergers and buyouts were already the order of the day in every business. For GM crops, however, the intervention of the big companies was unusual in that it brought together into multinationals parties that normally had little to do with one another: pharmaceuticals (as big brother), chemicals (smaller), and seeds (smallest). The first wave of mergers, which continued into 1998, resulted in six giant concerns—Monsanto and Novartis being the best known. Both of these corporations have since merged with other companies. So far, both sales figures and product development have been extremely positive: 1999 was an exceptionally good year for product sales, and figures for 2000 also look good. But the shareholders are starting to get cold feet.

The climate for investment in GM foods is not favorable. A dispassionate report on one major concern, DuPont, and on the GM food business in general, issued by Deutsche Bank in the summer of 1999, counseled caution in dealing in this kind of share.[15] The subtitle of the report echoes the usual response from Deutsche Bank's own shareholders: "Thanks, But No Thanks." The research institute responsible for the report recommended selling off shares in certain companies, holding on to stock in others, and, as a general word of advice, biding one's time and keeping a close eye on the market. This advice was not based on any reason to believe there was anything wrong with the products: "Although we are willing to believe that genetically modified organisms are safe and may provide a benefit for the environment, the perception wars are being lost by industry."

The multinationals' fiercest critics maintain that if stock values fall, these corporations are getting only what they deserve. They put their money into products of no relevance to consumers in their own wealthy markets, they rejected out of hand any idea of discussing the risks, and they actively resisted calls to provide better information to help consumers make up their minds on whether to opt for the new products or not. Indeed, the companies' overhasty, all-or-nothing approach has invited such criticism. More constructive thinking on the part of blasé multinational chief executive officers is long overdue, but even now they do not seem to be much wiser. "Nobody Will Help Monsanto" ran one headline. Neither retailers nor environmental organizations were willing to attend talks that would, according to the invitation, be behind closed doors and confidential.[16]

The tide turned against the GM food business with a vengeance in 1999. Offloading the new products on the world market became so difficult that non-GM crops became the better commodity investment, offering a better price for farmers. In the United States, where Bt maize has been such a huge success, the Environmental Protection Agency has found it necessary to underscore the importance of farmers' obeying the rules governing cultivation (such as providing refuges; see Chapter 2) to prevent a rapid escalation in pest resistance.[17] Also in the United States, projected mergers have been put on hold, and plans are now afoot to split up the industrial giants once again into their separate divisions, in part to ensure the pharmaceutical industry will not be made to suffer for its links with the conglomerates' controversial activities on the food front. As the DuPont report wisely pointed out, getting consumers to accept biotechnology in the agricultural sector is going to take longer than expected.[18]

The situation is clearly paradoxical. Farmers in the United States feel let down because they are not getting the prices they had hoped for, although they have benefited from the new crops that yield more for less outlay. In Brazil, there is a brisk traffic in GM soybean seeds, smuggled across the border from Argentina where GM varieties reign supreme. Farmers enjoy big savings when crops need to be sprayed with just one herbicide.[19]

This tricky situation is being exploited in a massive and lengthy lawsuit in the United States, in which farmers are seeking compensation from the seed producers for having been tricked into buying a product that has now been brought into disrepute. The suit is officially being brought on behalf of farmers in the United States and abroad who feel intimidated by the dominance of the big companies and by the contracts that have to be entered into in order to obtain the seed. But the instigators of this case and its financial backers—and litigation is an enormously costly business in the United States—appear to be private organizations opposed to genetic modification and with a solid tradition of raising money for various causes.[20]

It is opposition to the multinationals and the huge concentration of capital invested in GM organisms—rather than, as one might have predicted, potential environmental risks—that is an important driver of the lawsuit. No one with any legal acumen believes that damages will be awarded in this case. But it creates a great deal of trouble and expense for the accused company and provides a platform for organizations to voice their opposition to the multinationals—a surefire way of attracting money for the plaintiff's cause, not to mention plenty of media attention. Thus one might observe that certain groups are doing everything they can to undermine the credibility of the companies involved in GM plant technology and then, having by and large succeeded, are accusing them of not inspiring confidence.

The Ethical Angle

The questions surrounding the phasing in of GM plants deserve to be treated in a more serious manner than has so far been the case. A large number of initiatives on the Internet, articles in scientific journals and the popular press, reports from scientific committees in Europe and the United States, and public hearings instigated by the U.S. and European governments have helped bring about an informed and penetrating discussion of the matter.

A number of international sources have focused on the question of choice. What should we choose? What should we reject? What will be the consequences of our choices? And what processes should we adopt to ensure the best possible basis for reaching a decision? Central to these deliberations is the need to enter into the discussion sincerely—a requirement of the dialogue ethic—and to give both professional arguments and personal opinions a fair hearing. Equally important, we must recognize that decisions need to be taken actively, since passivity is also a choice, and that certain viewpoints and decisions may not meet the demands and expectations of all.

The process of choice can function on several levels, from the basic question of whether genetic engineering should be countenanced at all to decisions on individual issues: are we prepared to accept a given plant with specific properties being tested in our part of the world?

At a general level, one absolutely crucial question for many people is whether we are interfering too much in fundamental biological processes: "Are we playing God?" As mentioned earlier (see Chapter 2), the boundaries between what nature and what human intervention can accomplish appear to be more fluid than most of us would ever have thought. In response to the "playing God" argument, the point is made that if we assume human intelligence and creativity are God-given, then they are gifts that, like the talents in the New Testament parable, should be put to use in the service of humankind. If one does not consider genetic modification (of plants, since that is what we are talking about here) a good thing, however, we are back where we started.

In discussing this truly fundamental question, rooted in the religious convictions of a great many people, it is interesting to note that the Catholic Church, known for its conservatism, has accepted the genetic modification of plants. In the autumn of 1999, after two years of discussion and analytical studies, the Papal Academy for Life announced (with a "cautious yes") that genetic engineering processes on plants and animals lay within the bounds of acceptable human activity, but the cloning of human beings could not be endorsed.[21] Earlier in the year, in its capacity as one of the main Protestant denominations, the Church of England issued a statement based on the technical and theological aspects of the matter. Couched in much the same terms as the Vatican's recommendations, it states that "wisdom is unlikely to lie either in an unlimited exploitation or in total prohibition, but in a careful consideration of individual proposals. In this respect, genetic engineering does not seem very different from other types of scientific advance."[22] Then, later in 1999, the Church of England's Working Party for Ethical Investment issued a recommendation that the church should not rent out fields from its sizable lands in England for the trial cultivation of GM plants. The argument here, however, was entirely practical: the fear that, in the long run, the value of the land might drop if it were planted with the new crops, especially if vandals got in on the act, generating bad publicity.[23] Also taken into consideration was the church's wish to be a good neighbor and not to become embroiled in any possible environmental wrangles.

On the one hand, then, the individual will not necessarily receive much guidance on these questions—pro or con—from the ecclesiastical side. On the other hand, no pronounced fear of en-

croaching on divine territory has been expressed in theological circles. And this is not a topic on which one would expect many
church leaders to voice an opinion, for or against.

Another general aspect of the ethical question is the integrity
ethic: it considers issues related to the sanctity of life and the integrity of nature and the individual. Such a debate obviously cannot deal in absolute points of view, since for thousands of years humans have altered and exploited the natural world for their own
purposes, with greater or lesser degrees of brutality. In much of Europe, for example, these inroads have been so extensive that the
landscape has become almost completely built-up, with only a ves-
tige of natural countryside, in the original meaning of the term, remaining.

Which brings us back once again to the question of whether, on
this particular point of genetic modification, humankind is going
too far. It is difficult to maintain that the individual plant is sacro-
sanct, in the same way individual humans are considered to be, so
the question must be whether the natural world as a whole suffers
as a result of the use of GM crops. What we must remember here is
that a fair amount of the genetic material obtainable through genetic modification can be produced just as well (although more
slowly and more expensively) through traditional plant breeding.
Thus it seems only reasonable that deliberation on this topic
should be confined to those instances in which genes are, through
genetic modification techniques, transferred across species boundaries, such as from fish to plants. But many genomes are quite similar from one species to another, and the categories of many microorganisms, as we noted in Chapter 2, are fluid. Therefore, the
division into species becomes more a matter of pragmatism than a
decision based on elementary differences.

If one thinks in purely technological terms, the distinction between the genes of various species can seem very contrived. Genes
are, to a very large extent, identical, but located in different places
and activated in different ways. Imagine that someone asked,
"Would you live in a house built using a brick from a demolished

school?" Most people would probably reply, "Yes, why not? One brick is much like another." "A brick taken from a church?" would probably produce the same response. But "a brick from a crematorium or from an abattoir?" You can almost feel the hesitancy in the response. Researchers know only too well that the same response can be expected when questions arise about transferring a gene. Transfer from a buttercup to a turnip would be deemed pretty harmless. But what about transferring a gene from a cat or a human brain? It might well be "the same kind of brick," but it might raise the same response of distaste or of going against the "natural order" as using the brick from a crematorium.

One intriguing line of thought arising from recent genetic research, as we noted in Chapter 2, involves the theory that each individual higher organism contains a large number of genes for all sorts of qualities, but that most are "silent."[24] A gene from a cat, say—or from another well-charted species—could be used during the laboratory phase to help pinpoint a successful combination of qualities. After that, it would be a matter of finding the corresponding gene in the turnip and activating it—a solution bound to appeal to many people, because it gets round the problem of crossing species boundaries in the final product.

Misgivings about GM plant technology are most often expressed in the area referred to as the utility ethic: is it of any use to anything or anyone? If one felt uneasy or uncertain about these new technological possibilities, any lack of utility would tip the scales in favor of "thanks, but no thanks." But the utility ethic question works both ways: if there are appreciable benefits to be gained for humankind by employing the new technology, then the matter must be discussed seriously and some misgivings may have to be waived.

The point we want to make here is that if we consider the utility ethic, we must conclude that developing countries should make their own choice about whether or not to apply genetic modification to agriculture as one means of furthering their development and reducing poverty and malnutrition. And every choice made should involve a weighing of what is acceptable and what lies outside the bounds of what each society feels able to endorse. There is nothing radically new in this. With any luck, we will be able to have an unbiased discussion, without anyone vetoing in advance either the debate or the decisions that might be reached. That way, the dialogue can influence the agenda.

Ownership of the New Technology

One difficult aspect of using genetic modification in plants is that an essentially positive attitude toward "sensible" products can run into serious practical difficulties, because the technology and the products are normally tightly protected by various measures, primarily patents. So it is not simply a matter of sailing along, developing crops that seem ideal for particular lands or locations. On the contrary, if researchers and plant breeders set out to expand on advances that have already been made, they can expect to run into major problems and a great deal of expense.

Ownership of new developments may mean they cannot be used by anyone else, or that they can be used only if one pays a hefty license fee. If the protective measures applied only to a single, final product—for example, a variety of maize resistant to a company's weed killer—the problem would be straightforward enough. But patent laws allow a company to own both the resistance property—the gene or genes, once their function has been documented —and, even more exclusively, the techniques employed to identify, prepare, and integrate the property into a GM plant.

It is the private companies, of course, that have felt the need to protect their inventions. Because they have invested so much in the lengthy and costly work of developing new plants, they naturally want to recoup their investment by having a monopoly on their products for the duration of the patent, which is normally twenty years. The key to most GM plant technology and products lies in the private sector, which latched on to the freely available results of public research back in the 1970s and 1980s when they first caught the whiff of money. These companies then sank huge amounts of capital into their own development programs, with the express in-tent of taking discoveries to the patent stage. With buyouts and mergers, a single company can gain control of all the technologies developed in-house, but all companies need to buy or exchange protected techniques from one another.

Public research has reacted in three different ways. First, it may publish research findings as soon as they are known, thus making them freely available to everyone. Published results cannot be patented, since the very act of publishing them means they are no longer considered new if applications for patents are made. Second, the public research institute may apply for patents on its discoveries, so the institute has something to sell or "swap" and the rights to using the discovery can be dispensed either on license or free of charge. Third, researchers may enter into joint projects with private companies under agreements specifying who can use which findings and—most important for developing countries—where public research may freely use the products and techniques.

Researchers and plant breeders find themselves in the unwonted situation for scientists of not being able to stand on the backs of their predecessors—or, if they can, then only for a fee. Until 1970, the patenting of all or part of a living organism was uncommon, but today thousands of such patents are in existence, the majority of them in the United States. Europe has been lagging slightly in this regard, although patent laws are much the same on both sides of the Atlantic.

One cannot simply turn a blind eye to patent rights and go on working as one pleases. The world today is thoroughly bound up in international agreements and we have to respect the ownership of inventions, trademarks, artistic copyrights, and so on; breaches of these rights are punishable under international sanctions. In practice, this system works rather differently from country to country, as we know from the large-scale piracy of brand-name clothes in certain parts of Asia. But for plants, a number of successful appeals have been brought, and now that the World Trade Organization (WTO) is gaining more clout, opting out of the protection system is becoming almost impossible.

Patents are national in nature and the protection is valid only in countries where the patent has been granted. Taking out patents can be expensive and is usually limited to those countries expected to offer promising markets. Many developing countries are therefore not targeted for patenting. Furthermore, many developing countries do not grant patents for living organisms. All members of the WTO have agreed to provide patent legislation for microorganisms, but they need not do so for other living organisms. Where patents have not been granted, researchers are free to develop technology patented elsewhere and governments are able to approve commercialization of technology for farmers. Except for the rules about microorganisms, countries can comply with WTO rules through other property regulations, including plant variety protection (PVP) regulations. But this protection covers only the marketing side, prohibiting other seed producers from cultivating a particular variety in order to sell the seed. Unlike under patents, researchers and breeders can further develop the new material and obtain the rights to the refined variety—if approved by the authorizing body. And there is one other vital detail: farmers must be allowed the traditional practice of saving some of their harvest to use as seed the following season.

The international debate on one question is fierce: just how much can be covered by patents? Under the twenty-year patent system, if a company is unwilling to exchange technology with others, or to issue licenses, this can create serious bottlenecks, particularly when extensive patents are granted on large portions of a plant's genome or on a comprehensive general technique. The trend today is more toward ensuring that patent rights are not too sweeping, and several U.S. lawsuits have succeeded in limiting the scope of patents.[25]

The situation remains tricky. Public research in countries where patents for living organisms are common has difficulty making progress, even when the professional expertise is at hand. And even when the money can be found, starting up a research project can involve complex legal juggling, since contracts often include individual genes and many different pieces of technology, permission for which has to be released by a succession of owners. In this one instance, we can view corporate buyouts as a good thing, because they have reduced the number of contractors.

We are now beginning to see some cases in which private companies are freely donating rights to researchers in the developing world. And occasionally we hear about multinationals that award training grants and wealthy laboratories that pass on research findings to their poorer counterparts. In general, though, research groups can make use of other people's findings only if they have the cash or something to give in exchange.

As is generally acknowledged, some sort of ownership protection is necessary if private enterprise is to invest in research. The question is whether this needs to be the blanket protection provided by patents or whether some more limited arrangement such as PVP regulations might not suffice. Private companies have not been all that keen on departing from the patents solution. But too dogged an insistence on exclusive rights and a reluctance to issue licenses can violate a country's antitrust laws to the point where national authorities can intervene with a court injunction making the issuing of licenses compulsory.

It is ironic that some of the organizations opposed to genetic modification in agriculture in the developing countries also lambaste the big companies for taking out patents, when the system of patents and the insistence on getting a return on the capital invested pretty much guarantee a slow and limited spread of modern developments in agriculture to the developing countries.

This slow progress may indeed be the outcome unless we can come up with an international agenda capable of smoothing the road and pushing changes through. Under this agenda, it would be ethically untenable for private companies to claim that new discoveries, based on publicly funded research and rooted in the plant-breeding efforts of generations of farmers, must show a profit in markets that have little purchasing power.

7 · MOVING FORWARD

Handle with Care

Decades have passed since the days when one could be unreservedly enthusiastic about technology, as were the first users of the phonograph, the telephone, or the electric lightbulb. But the fear of technology has always been there, lurking in the shadow of inventions, as the great French scientist Louis Pasteur discovered. His technique for killing harmful microorganisms in foods without damaging the foods themselves was called a tool of the devil and provoked some heated public debate,[1] before being seen for what it was: a genuine scientific advance.

Today, even the most enthusiastic biotechnologist frequently reminds us that genetic engineering, like other tools, can be used sensibly or irresponsibly. A comparison is often drawn with the age-old discovery of fire,[2] calling to mind the subject of a school essay that once, many years ago, blighted a class of students' entire Easter vacation: "Fire—Friend or Foe?" Our guess is that while most of the hapless essay writers could see the pitfalls of fire, they found it hard to imagine a life without it. Such an essay probably included warnings against letting children play with matches or leaving burning candles near the Christmas tree. Still, it is a good bet that most of the essays arrived at the same conclusion: "But, handled with care, fire can be. . . ."

And that is just how we view the potential of genetic engineering to help the farmers of developing countries. But the catalog of expectations as to what constitutes "handling with care" is somewhat more complex than that for fire. We can divide it into general requirements for technology and its uses and specific requirements for the application of genetic engineering to the conditions in developing countries. Here we discuss the general and specific requirements together.

Free and Informed Choice

From the moment the first genetically modified crops appeared on the market, the effort to treat GM products as a special case looked like a losing battle. The major companies completely ignored demands to label products containing GM ingredients. In the United States, authorities saw the need for labeling only if a product contained substances or qualities one would not normally expect to find in that product—for example, a peanut gene in a soybean, which might trigger an allergic reaction in some consumers, or a different nutritional content. The dismissive attitude of the manufacturers could be attributed to their thinking it a contradiction to treat as a special case goods that were, in the words of the U.S. Food and Drug Administration, "substantially identical" to already known products, such as the maize in cornflakes or the soy in bread products. This, of course, left manufacturers wide open to the obvious rejoinder, "Well, if there's no problem with these goods, why don't you want to declare them on food labels?" (This sounds much like the classic argument between advocates of openness and secrecy in politics and administration.) And as long as a reasonably large majority felt happy about these new goods, one could get away with saying there was no need for labeling.

The dismissive attitude of the producers was prompted mainly by a number of concrete practical problems. After all, to farmers, maize is maize and soybeans are soybeans, especially if there are no visible differences between one variety and the next. So during the first years of GM crops, it was common practice to throw together

GM and non-GM seeds in one great mishmash. With labeling requirements, either the mixture as a whole would have to be labeled as genetically modified or the varieties would have to be separated. And while individual farmers could easily manage the job of keeping them apart, the grain elevators, mills, and factories that processed the crops would have to be very careful to keep the different varieties separate from start to finish.

This would certainly create extra work and cost a great deal, but it could be done. In the move to quash this demand, however, U.S. manufacturers stressed the difficulties and the resulting price increases they would have to pass on to their customers. But in Europe, where labeling of the few GM products on the market was compulsory, the separation of the different varieties proved a practical possibility. In January 2000, at the meeting in Montreal of the Biodiversity Convention (a follow-up to the Earth Summit held in Rio de Janeiro in 1992), the labeling of commodities for export was recognized as a universal requirement: many countries simply want to know whether crops have been genetically modified. The aim now is to come up with a permissible proportion of GM seeds per load that does not affect the purity of a crop. In all probability countries will settle on 1 to 2 percent, bearing in mind that vacuuming silos and cargo holds completely clear of every single seed left over from harvest to harvest or from trip to trip would be very difficult.

In the United States, the labeling issue took on a new dimension when exporters began to demand products that could be guaranteed free of GM components. Prices for GM maize and soybeans dropped slightly, and even though they were cheaper for the farmers to produce, in a number of cases the profit was less than on non-GM varieties. Today many countries expect products containing GM ingredients to be labeled as such, enabling consumers to decide whether or not to purchase them.

There is another side to the labeling issue. Some people support "blanket labeling" that also indicates whether genetic engineering has been used at any stage in the processing of the product, regardless of whether traces of GM ingredients can be identified. This is much like differentiating between eggs from hens in cages and eggs from free-range hens. For some consumers, detailed information on how the eggs have been produced is a selling point, even though there is no proof of any difference in the nutritional value or health-promoting qualities of the two types of eggs. But some see this as an ethical, not a nutritional, issue.

For these two types of consumer information, it is clear who has responsibility for what. The state must evaluate the risks to consumers and take responsibility for labeling products having ingredients that could be damaging to health. However, labels giving details of the production process could be the manufacturer's responsibility, with the state ensuring that the labeling conforms to set standards and provides proper information. This is required so as to avoid any risk of misrepresentation or the sort of confusion that resulted from the introduction of various types of labeling for organic foods or goods considered environmentally friendly (eco-labeling). In the case of GM foods, the market will most likely see a diverse range of products bearing compulsory labels where required and supplemented by producers' voluntary consumer information, for which some sections of the buying public will be happy to pay a bit extra.

Political moves toward mandatory labeling of all foods that have been associated with genetic engineering at some point in the production process would make it difficult to avoid the labeling of cheese, beer, bakery products, and other goods, because genetic modification is generally involved in some stage of the processing. This question of what constitutes comprehensive labeling highlights the issue of how one defines the "norm." Advocates of blanket labeling maintain that it should also apply to livestock raised on feed mixes containing a certain amount of GM feed, even though the contents of the feed are broken down in the animals' digestive process. And that requirement, so farmers estimate, would cover all the larger domestic animals in the developed world, except those raised organically. And what about oil from GM maize? Maize oil contains no DNA and therefore no modified genes!

Blanket labeling would lead to higher prices for food that may contain GM substances or may have been in touch with GM substances during the production process. Some might find it more reasonable to pass on the costs of labeling to those consumers who are looking for assurances that their food contains nothing that has been genetically modified, as is already the case with organic products. The labeling condition would thus be imposed on another group of manufacturers: nonorganic producers who can guarantee that their products involve no GM crops or ingredients and no genetic engineering techniques in the production process. This might well turn out to be as complicated as it sounds. In the short term, the regulations could stipulate that all food labels should state that "genetic modification has/has not been involved at some point in the production of this item." The authorities will have to seriously consider which, if any, approach is tenable.

Consumer Information: More than Labeling

To be effective, a labeling system should be based on sufficient information to permit consumers to make choices based on their values and desires. Government health warnings on tobacco products make good sense, because consumers are so well informed that, generally speaking, they know what they are choosing or refusing to buy. But things are not so clear-cut for organically produced foods and other products. The general feeling is that the organic production process has been good for the environment and has helped save some natural resources. But most people probably also assume that foods bearing an "organically grown and processed" label are better for their health than are nonorganic foods. And here we are faced with a more debatable assertion, one that is currently being explored to see whether it has any solid foundation in fact. So, as yet, customers have no guarantee that the label is saying what they think it is saying.

For GM foods, consumers in general have nothing like the knowledge necessary to decipher what a label is actually telling them. Any labeling system must therefore be backed up by much more information than is available at the moment. Consumer organizations do what they can, but in the main their messages attract broad public attention only when, in tandem with environmental organizations, they issue statements on specific cases that are of interest to the press. These statements tend not to raise the general standard of information, because most efforts by these groups and the responding industries involve accusations, denials, rejections, and warnings.

In an enlightened climate, informative labels make good sense, although one ought not to expect any really dramatic consumer shifts as a result. Standards and descriptions are bound to reflect the society in which the products are used. That being so, we cannot assume that what people in industrialized countries expect to learn from labels can be transferred to the same type of product in a developing country, where quality standards may be closer to those deemed acceptable in the industrialized world fifty years ago.

This is not to suggest, of course, that substandard products should be dumped on developing countries. It is a fact of life, however, that people's tolerance thresholds or acceptable-risk levels are greatly affected by their income levels. Shopping bags in the supermarket of a prosperous city suburb are not filled with the same goods as are those in a poorer inner-city district. For example, the selection of food items and quality grades depends on whether a household spends 5 percent or 30 percent of its income on food. In developing countries, 80 percent of the family's income may be spent on food, and risk reductions causing food price increases may not be of interest, particularly if the risks are virtual rather than real.

The Right to Say No

The resolution passed by the Montreal Biodiversity Convention in January 2000 concerned labeling and choice in an even more radical context. It represented the provisional end to a lengthy and ac-rimonious battle over the extent to which free-trade regulations or policy decisions should reign supreme in a global context. The large grain-producing countries in the West, in particular Argentina, Canada, and the United States, could not see why government authorities should be entitled to specific information on the contents of a load of imported maize or soybeans and why they should have the right to refuse GM commodities. They argued that the principles of free trade had already been established under the WTO. Given that GM and non-GM commodities are considered "substantially identical," such a refusal, they argued, is simply a technical barrier to trade, unacceptable under the terms of the WTO agreement.

It was a hard-fought battle. In the end, a handful of the major grain-exporting countries that opposed compulsory labeling, called the Miami Group, were at odds with most of the rest of the world, including a coalition of such unlikely bedfellows as the European Union, Japan, and a number of developing countries. The outcome was that any country had the right to refuse GM crops, if it was uncertain about the consequences of importing them. Such uncertainty might concern adverse effects on consumers' health or—the worry most often expressed by developing countries—on the environment. Although most of the imported GM grain would be consumed as food, some countries feared that some of it might be lost in the wild or used as seed on farms, thus creating the risk of inadvertent crossing with local crops or the wild flora.

This issue is closely bound up with biosafety, which deals with the responsible handling of living organisms to prevent the risk of accidents. Biosafety was set firmly on the agenda after the 1992 Rio de Janeiro summit. Although the resolutions passed by the conference were not endorsed on paper by every country, they now form the rules, national and international, on how to manage the countryside, agriculture, fishing, and forestry. The chances of these good intentions being pursued depend heavily on the political will both within individual countries and at the international level.

Slowly but steadily the agreements are being implemented in a number of countries. But many countries face the purely practical problem of finding enough professional expertise to monitor the situation and make sure the rules are obeyed, as well as a lack of appropriate institutions. In this respect, many of the smaller developing countries are at a disadvantage, and it is therefore important that they should be able to refuse an import without having to present an encyclopedia of scientific arguments. If they cannot gauge whether a particular crop might entail specific risks for their country, with its particular natural environment and form of agriculture, they should be able to say no. So the Montreal convention's ruling was exactly what this group of countries needed.

Where biotechnology is concerned, no country is starting completely from scratch. But many poorer countries are weak in scientific and technological expertise because they invest far less in research and development than do the wealthy countries. We can find isolated pockets of brilliant specialist research in a number of developing countries, including those of southern Africa, but in the main only the larger developing countries, such as Brazil, China, Egypt, India, and South Africa, are conducting the really solid research. These scientifically strong countries have embarked on biotechnology research in a big way, including testing and production of GM crops. This has required the passage of legislation and regulations covering testing, monitoring, and safety. Both the research and the administration sides are now up and running, so these countries can enter into international collaborations with the multinationals and apply genetic modification techniques to agriculture.

In many smaller countries, though, neither the legislation nor the administration has yet reached a stage where they can enter into collaborations or develop GM crops for themselves. So one obvious regulation has to be that no experimentation should be carried out in these countries. In any case, such a move would probably be the kiss of death for the reputation of any company that tried to do so, a fact that the multinationals fully appreciate. We have seen no instances of a developing country being used as a test field without its full consent and without the firm conviction that it was professionally equipped to reach such a decision.

The requirement for decent conduct might seem self-evident, and a list of more wide-ranging demands for the biotechnology industry as it relates to developing countries has also been drawn up. For example, a training program should be set up for researchers from developing countries that will bring them to the forefront of biotechnology, giving their countries the expertise necessary to evaluate the new possibilities.[3] A few private companies have financed such programs, and in the short term the public image of these companies would be much enhanced if they were to systematically put aside money for more of the same. In the longer term this would improve the chances for these companies to collaborate with countries that otherwise would remain blank spots on their marketing maps while at the same time strengthening the expertise of the developing countries.

Extermination of a Terminator

Another requirement for "handling with care" in GM plant technology results from a new plant property developed by some of the large genetic engineering companies: plants that produce sterile seeds that do not sprout after harvesting. When the patent was taken out on the technique, which was developed in a collaboration between private and public research in the United States, its originators were convinced they had found a brilliant technical solution to two annoying problems: the GM characteristics would not spread in the wild and farmers would have to buy seed every season. Thus the reduction of a potential environmental risk and protection of the ownership of the technology were taken care of in one go.

Sterile seeds have consequences. With traditional crops, after harvesting, some seeds—say maize seeds or seed potatoes—can be set aside for use at the start of the next season. However, seeds and seed potatoes bring in a better price than do grain or potatoes sold at the barn door, so seed producers are not keen on farmers' saving seed. Setting aside seed for next year may be expressly forbidden under the rules of a contract covering patented crops. And sterile seeds, of course, make such rules unnecessary. This is no big deal in the wealthier countries, where farmers generally prefer to buy fresh seed every year: new seed carries less risk of disease, has probably been treated against fungi and mold, and comes with a guarantee that it will sprout. In addition, for hybrids, second-generation seeds do not produce nearly as good a yield as the first. Farmers in developing countries, however, do save seeds for sowing the next season, simply because they cannot afford to buy new seeds every year—this is the case for 80 percent of farmers in the developing world.[4] It is impossible to distinguish between a GM and non-GM seed without specialized testing equipment, and saving seeds for next year's harvest that may prove sterile could be disastrous for farm families and even for whole villages, because farmers in developing countries commonly lend or sell seeds to their neighbors.

For a while, the seed producers tended to ignore this detail, but it elicited such a strong response from public development research and nongovernmental organizations, which came up with the epithet "terminator gene," that the patent holders have laid down their arms, at least for the time being. In a statement issued in the fall of 1999, after a whole summer of dispute, Monsanto announced that for the next five-year period it would not seek approval of any material that included terminator genes.[5] One of the conditions imposed on the industry, therefore, should be a mandatory requirement that this "terminator" technology should not turn up later in crop seeds produced for use in the developing countries. In the industrialized countries the situation does not pose much of a problem, partly because the level of information is generally higher and partly because, as noted above, the reusing of harvested seeds has gradually been phased out.

Corporate Profits

No one who has followed the development of genetic modification in agriculture can be in any doubt that the private sector is driven by the possibility of making a tidy profit. Years of work and millions of dollars go into the development of a marketable product. And along the way, as in any research, investigators come up against many a dead end and scrap many a half-baked prototype that has come to nothing. Even when a company does end up with a successful product, it still cannot be sure of recouping its investment. Authorizations can be withdrawn, as is happening in the European Union; proceedings can be suspended, as has been the case with the E.U. moratorium on new approvals; or approval can be denied, as has happened in the United States. So when a product does eventually make its way onto the market, it has to bring in some profit. This is why producers take such a hard line on the need for patents and on protecting themselves through contracts with farmers and checks to prevent any abuse.

Seen in this light the terminator ploy seemed quite logical, but it is not the way forward for developing countries. Consideration is being given to employing somewhat less radical methods of protecting a company's investment and the environment. Say, for instance, that a producer develops a sturdy high-yielding maize plant that can also tolerate a certain plant disease if the seeds are treated with a harmless chemical developed by the same company. Such a variety will attract interest from many quarters, certainly in some developing countries. Farmers who can afford to do so will buy the new maize seeds and the appropriate volume of chemicals to activate disease protection if and when necessary. After harvesting, seed can be set aside for the next season, if the farmer so wishes. But the built-in protection will come into play next season only if the chemical is also used, and this is how the company makes its profit. Farmers will not be buying a pig in a poke; they will get exactly what they pay for: a sturdy high-yielding maize that can be reused but does not spread its new properties to the environment.

From an ethical point of view, such a variety of maize would not present the same problems as the terminator technique. Undoubtedly, there would be some complaint, and we would hear some rumblings on the day this proposal was put into effect in the developing world. But before raising immediate objections, one must accept that agriculture is a business; money, not philanthropy, calls the shots. And public research could not possibly manage to do all the development work necessary.

There is no way that all hopes can be fulfilled. The GM rice with beta-carotene—the golden rice developed by public research with funding from private philanthropic foundations and freely available for further breeding by individual countries—seems to be a splendid addition to the diet of poor people. But, on behalf of those same people, Christian Aid has rejected such synthetic discoveries.[6] The poor would do better to eat a varied diet, this group argues, then there would be no problem. It fails to tell us, however, how these people should find, let alone pay for, this varied diet. The knee-jerk response of NOAH, a Danish nongovernmental organization (NGO), was to back up this criticism of golden rice by declaring that private companies are out simply to line their own pockets.[7] It is interesting to note that this rice was developed by the public sector and that all patent holders have granted free access to the components included in its development. In this respect, too, it seems reasonable to make the requirement that, rather than making sweeping judgments about GM foods based on the motives of the developers and distributors, we address each case on its merits, its actual, inherent advantages and disadvantages to the potential recipients.

The environmental NGOs have taken a negative view of GM foods from the start, and many NGOs with a developing-world focus have backed them up in this, some more categorically than others. We find it deeply disturbing that private organizations with an honorable record of setting high standards and prompting Western society to be concerned about the food and agriculture in developing countries, to support them both morally and materially, should be so blind to the potential of genetic modification to help the world's poor feed themselves. They seem to have closed their eyes and their minds, allowing their skepticism about the involvement of private companies to completely dominate and overshadow some of the promising elements of the new technology. This is particularly unfortunate because the technology can be developed by the public sector and made available to poor farmers at little or no cost.

Not that the private companies make it any easier. But surely the NGOs, in all their diversity, could approach this topic with a more open mind, could analyze the possibilities, each according to its own merits. And indeed, a more nuanced attitude and an openness to dialogue are beginning to emerge among some of the private development organizations.[8] By adopting such a stance, the NGOs could without doubt become a valuable pressure group—one that is not simply dismissive but uses its clout to help realize the potential of genetic engineering for the smallholders of the developing world.

And if the private companies could relax their restrictions just a little, creating a more general openness to the further development and use of genetic modification, they could be persuaded that the patents system is too sweeping in its protection of their rights in developing countries. The rights system that operates under the auspices of the WTO offers another option specifically for plants: the plant variety protection system (see Chapter 6), which has long been an international norm and is still, in most countries, the only system. Patenting, on the other hand, functions more as a sort of rental arrangement for farmers: the right to cultivate a crop from patented seeds is rented for a fee and the harvested crop can be sold for consumption but cannot be replanted without a fee. This is similar to buying, or "licensing," a computer software program: as with computer software, the buyer cannot develop the patented plant further and then sell the improved product; but with the software, at least we can still reuse it on our own machines.

Another requirement, therefore, is for multinationals to acknowledge that they can get by with less than patenting and can cover themselves with the solid guarantees of the PVP system, which has up to now ensured excellent profits for the seed producers. The companies could do as a few already have done: grant licenses *en masse* to researchers and agriculture in the developing countries. The release of key pieces of technology—such as one of the protected techniques for the transfer of genes from one organism to another—for use in developing countries would also be a positive move.

We are now hearing calls for such steps from all sides,[9] and in the long term the big companies would do well to heed them. Corporate mergers and buyouts have created such massive conglomerates that government authorities in some countries may begin to demand the disbanding of these monopolies. The more provocatively a monopoly is run, the greater the risk of the state's intervening. After years of turning a deaf ear to the dialogue on alternatives to patenting, the industry would be wise to pay a little more attention.

You Can Never Be Too Careful

In the overcautious civil service of an earlier day, obsessed as it was with not making mistakes, "you can never be too careful" was an unofficial motto in many countries. And on the whole mistakes were avoided, although, as one might expect, advances were also thin on the ground. Today, a different sort of balance has been struck in most sectors of society between progress and safety, but we also have the knowledge and control mechanisms that increase the demand for something close to absolute insurance against risk, without any slackening of the pace.

In February 2000 the German authorities decided to rescind authorization of a GM maize variety, because it had been developed with the aid of a marker gene resistant to a certain group of antibiotics (this type of marker gene was chosen for its usefulness in the laboratory during the research stage; see Chapter 2). A number of countries have refused to grant marketing permits on this maize,

on the grounds of uncertainty about the risk of antibiotic resistance giving rise to resistant bacteria that cause human disease.

It is difficult to obtain any watertight guarantee that this type of
marker gene carries no health risks. The crops have been on the
market for some years now and no problems have been identified.
But scientific doubts have been raised, and analysts have established the theoretical chances of a problem arising. So, for some
years now, both private and public researchers have been working
on ways of eliminating this type of marker from the finished product. One way is to remove the antibiotic marker after the development work is completed and before the new plant goes on the
market. This is a rather complex exercise and is not cheap, but it
can be done. The other method is to develop other, harmless
markers. These are now finding their way into the laboratory and
will soon be a standard part of the process. Use of private firms'
patented markers will obviously cost money, and even the markers
developed through publicly funded research will probably contain
a certain element of privately owned technology, which means
these, too, will entail some outlay.

In such a situation, companies that hold the rights to techniques
involving antibiotic-resistance markers might be inclined to carry
on using this technology because it costs them nothing. Therefore,
regulations will have to be put into effect to shelve the first generation of marker genes. Varieties already on the market will probably
have to be modified, with the new type of marker replacing the
old; otherwise these older varieties will be impossible to sell when
better products are to be had, as the German response has shown.

Higher Priority to Social Utility

Unless we utterly reject the idea of genetic modification in agriculture as a matter of principle, we have to admit that, for the developing countries, it does present some favorable opportunities.
These exciting prospects, however, will not come to fruition on
their own. The market will not develop and deliver the goods if
there is no one to buy them. In the best of all possible worlds, ef-

fective state systems would supplement the market by supplying what is needed for the common good, which in this case is solid agricultural research.

In most developing countries the state infrastructure is weak and underfinanced and can supply little in the way of services. To compensate for such failings, a number of international public systems have been set up, among them the Consultative Group on International Agricultural Research centers. The CGIAR has an annual budget of around 350 million U.S. dollars—not a huge amount of money by the time it is divided among sixteen centers conducting research on agricultural crops, livestock, fisheries, agroforestry, food policy, and systems for the preservation of plant genes. The CGIAR also offers support to developing countries for setting up their own research institutes—another area of expenditure. Approximately 20 percent of each center's budget goes toward training researchers in developing countries. Each of the centers involved in crop breeding spends the lion's share of its money on traditional agricultural research. On an international plane, this represents just a tiny fraction of the funds that any one of the big biotechnology companies has at its disposal. Thus the public and private sectors are by no means working on equal terms, even though researchers in some wealthy countries are working on crops for the developing countries. So one obvious requirement would be for the wealthy part of the world to make a bigger investment in agricultural research in the developing countries. By increasing its contribution to international agricultural research and using its enormous pool of expertise, the industrialized world could ensure that genetic modification will eventually fulfill some of its promise for feeding the poor.

The developing countries could also reap direct, relevant benefits from private research by way of a tender system. A group of aid organizations could band together to identify a crucial agricultural problem in, say, Africa—leaf mosaic, for example, the scourge of the cassava plant. Leaf mosaic is a virus spread by minute insects, and so far it has been almost impossible to combat. Stamping out leaf mosaic for good would be a great boon to poor farmers and consumers, because cassava is important in the diet of many low-income people and it can thrive even in poor soil and with unreliable rainfall. The virus and its spread could be combated by rendering the plants resistant to viral attack, which would probably require a number of genes to prevent resistance from breaking down too rapidly. This is an expensive and complicated exercise calling for modern equipment, specialist knowledge, and access to the very latest technology. Few developing countries could manage to carry out such a task within a reasonable time frame, and certainly not the African countries plagued by leaf mosaic. Guided by specialists, the aid organizations could calculate the full scope of such an undertaking and organize a "competition" for the development of a high-yielding cassava plant that is resistant to leaf mosaic. The prize would have to cover the likely costs of the development work plus a substantial premium corresponding to the normal return on agricultural research. The competition could be open to both private and public bodies, possibly in collaboration, but there would be just one prize for coming up with a successful result. The new plant would thereafter become public property, available for further development and adaptation to local conditions and subsequently available free to all small-scale farmers.

Similar ideas have been bandied about for the development of a malaria vaccine,[10] another good example of a pressing and enormous problem facing the developing countries for which a technical solution could surely be found if only the funding were available.

Slow and Steady Wins the Race

The outcry elicited by the hasty launching of GM foods onto an unprepared market has certainly taught the major seed producers an expensive lesson. Even the best discoveries—and these particular ones were not in that category—need time to be accepted. Instead, the companies' hell-for-leather approach has turned what could have been a case-by-case discussion into an all-out, all-embracing confrontation for or against genetic modification. As such, the debate bears little resemblance to the model normally employed in addressing vital concerns in a compromise-oriented democratic society. One of our essential aims must be to get back to a reasonable form of debate. Not every kind of genetic engineering is justifiable and not every risk scenario is relevant in every case.

Much harm has been done to the debate by the bundling together of a number of different agendas. When biologists argue the scientific aspects of the matter (and of course, they do not all see eye to eye), their arguments are met by denunciations of the multinationals' monopolization and concentration of capital. When attention is drawn to the food deficit in developing countries, out come the statistics to prove there is plenty to eat if only the food were distributed evenly across the globe. Arguments about the dispersal risk of GM maize in Mexico are used as a line of attack against using potatoes with an inbuilt resistance to pests in Denmark!

Obviously we cannot start the discussion again from scratch, ignoring all the dust already stirred up. But we could follow a piece of good advice from researchers working at the Royal Danish Veterinary and Agricultural University: "Turnips on their own, rape on its own."[11] What they are getting at is that (in Denmark, at least) the risks of crossbreeding with wild varieties are very different for these two crops: the fodder turnips now being cultivated in test fields are biennials harvested before they flower; rape is an annual. So the precautions that need to be taken with GM turnips are not necessarily the same as those that apply to rape, under Danish conditions. This piece of advice also has a broader application, of course: considerations that may be relevant in one context cannot be allowed to dictate the rules in another, quite different context. Such a mistake could lead to both too little and too much regulation and control, if what we are left with is some sort of standard package. For example, Danish experts have had such serious reservations about the possible crossing of GM rape with local weeds that a GM variety ready to be marketed has now been shelved, for the time being at least. Similar concerns about GM potatoes might be valid for Peru but would be pointless for Denmark, because potatoes have no wild relatives in Denmark.

An approach to genetic modification based on a case-by-case evaluation, as practiced in E.U. authorization procedures, is a reasonable requirement to set. And such an approach would undoubtedly enhance the objectivity of the entire debate and reduce the chance of several different agendas becoming mixed up. All issues can be discussed, with or without consensus; but they ought to be kept apart. The political aspects of dependency and monopolization, for example, go far beyond genetic modification to the broader issue of globalization. The limits to human manipulation of God's creations is another aspect that can be discussed independently. The argument about organic versus traditional agriculture would be an ideal subject for a general debate on what we expect from tomorrow's agriculture. Social utility is an issue in itself, for all countries. Then comes the problem of resolving all the technical risk factors, which is undeniably a job for the specialists. In the public debate, the need for a certain amount of professional wherewithal to decide specific points about the risks of the new technology is still not fully accepted. This is due in part to a general distrust of new technology and the competence and integrity of both government authorities and private companies.

Free Choice for Everyone—Us and Them

On a Saturday morning, for those standing in line at the checkout in their local supermarket in Europe or the United States, an adequate food supply appears to be anything but a problem. They see not only plenty of food but also an overwhelming variety of products, brands, and qualities. What more could one ask for? It is easy to dismiss the notion that there is any need for GM products. If such products do find their way onto grocery store shelves, shoppers certainly do not have to pop them into their shopping carts. But can a strong case be made for stopping others from doing so?

We, the authors of this book, do not believe the arguments

against genetic modification are strong enough to dictate that the world should stop any further development of GM plants. And we find it extremely worrying that a minority that has more than enough to eat should make life so difficult for those who do not. Potential public and private investors, facing a vociferous and hostile response from some quarters, may well decide that the only easy and logical solution is to discount the use of genetic engineering technology in food production and focus exclusively on its use in human medicine. Society may be turning its back on some possible advances, but we, the well-fed of the world, will get by just the same.

The developing countries, with the possible exception of China, will have no chance to benefit from GM food research unless they can draw on knowledge and contacts in the wealthy part of the world. If the continuation of research in the donor countries—those that invest, through aid contributions, in development-oriented public international research—is deemed unacceptable, the international research groups will have to stand by as the funding dries up. And researchers in the developed world will naturally turn their attention to areas for which funding is available.

Traditional agricultural research will carry on as before, and, as before, good results will regularly be forthcoming. But not at the rate, or of the innovative nature, that is clearly needed. How, in all conscience, can the well-fed of the world, by turning what should be a choice into a global dictate, opt out of the new technologies that could provide the opportunity for all the world's people to be well-fed?

NOTES

The following abbreviations are used in the notes: CIMMYT, Centro Internacional de Mejoramiento de Maiz y Trigo (International Maize and Wheat Improvement Center); IFPRI, International Food Policy Research Institute. Short titles are used for cited works after the first citation.

Introduction

1. Mae-Wan Ho, *Genetic Engineering Dream or Nightmare? Turning the Tide on the Brave New World of Bad Science and Big Business* (London: Continuum, 2000).

2. Lord Melchett, "GM Crops Worse Than N-waste," *Guardian* (Manchester), September 6, 2000.

3. Robert B. Shapiro, *The Welcome Tension of Technology: The Need for Dialogue about Agricultural Biotechnology,* CEO Series no. 37 (St. Louis, Mo.: Center for the Study of American Business, Washington University, 2000).

4. Nuffield Council on Bioethics, *Genetically Modified Crops: The Ethical and Social Issues* (London: Nuffield Foundation, 1999).

5. "Gener Spredes i Naturen [Genes are spreading in the wild]," *Politiken* (Denmark), September 12, 1999.

6. Mira Shiva and Vandana, "India's Human Guinea Pigs: Human vs. Property Rights," *Science as Culture* 2 no. 10 (2000): 59-81.

7. Christina Aid, "Selling Suicide," at <www.christian-aid.org/uk/reports/suicide/summary>, accessed September 23, 1999.

8. Ibid.

9. S. Rampton and J. Stanber, *Trust Us, We're Experts: How Industry Manipulates Science and Gambles with Your Future* (New York: Jeremy P. Tarcker/Putnam, 2000).

10. Cyrus G. Ndiritu, "Biotechnology in Africa: Why the Controversy?" in *Agricultural Biotechnology and the Poor*, ed. G. J. Persley and M. M. Lantin (Washington, D.C.: Consultative Group on International Agricultural Research, 2000).

11 Hassan Adamu, "We'll Feed Our People as We See Fit," *Washington Post*, September 11, 2000.

12. Søren Kolstrup, "Kan Generne Trækkes Tilbage? [Can the genes be pulled back?]," *Information* (Denmark), November 8, 1999.

13. Ndiritu, "Biotechnology in Africa."

14. Birger Lindberg Møller, "Genteknologiens Betydning for Fremtidens Fødevareproduktion [The importance of genetic technology in future food production]," in *Gensplejsede Fødevarer* (Copenhagen: Teknologirådet, 1999), 59.

Chapter 1. Agricultural Research

1. Donald L. Plucknett, *Science and Agricultural Transformation*, International Food Policy Research Institute Lecture Series no. 1 (Washington, D.C.: IFPRI, 1993). *Tons* here and throughout the book refers to metric tons.

2. Ibid.

3. Throughout this book the cereal crop *Zea mays* is referred to as *maize* rather than *corn*, as it is known is the United States.

4. Peter B. Hazell and C. Ramasamy, *The Green Revolution Reconsidered* (Baltimore: Johns Hopkins University Press, for IFPRI, 1991).

5. CIMMYT, *CIMMYT Annual Report 1994* (Mexico City: CIMMYT, 1995).

6. Consultative Group for International Agricultural Research, Technical Advisory Committee (TAC), "Environment Impact of the CGIAR: An Assessment" (Rome: TAC/Food and Agriculture Organization of the United Nations, April 2001).

7. CIMMYT, *Annual Report 1994*.

8. Gordon Conway, *The Doubly Green Revolution: Food for All in the Twenty-first Century* (Ithaca, N.Y.: Cornell University Press, 1998).

9. CIMMYT, *A Sampling of CIMMYT Impacts, 1998* (Mexico City: CIMMYT, 1999).

10. United Nations Population Fund, newsletter, September 23, 1999.

Chapter 2. The Expanding Boundaries of Research

1. Søren Molin, "Biologiens Paradoxer [The paradoxes of biology]," annex to *Erhvervsministeriets Debatoplæg: De Genteknologiske Valg* [Debate: the genetic technology choices] (Copenhagen: Ministry of Industry, 1999).

2. David Baltimore, "Our Genome Unveiled," *Nature* 409 (February 15, 2001): 814-16.

3. This theory is outlined in "When Did Rice Become Corn?" *International Herald Tribune*, March 3, 2000.

4. "Scientists Weed Danger out of GM Crops," *Times* (London), November 16, 1999.

5. Møller, "Genteknologiens Betydning."

6. Samuel B. Lehrer, "Potential Health Risks of Genetically Modified Organisms: How Can Allergens Be Assessed and Minimized?" in *Agricultural Biotechnology and the Poor*, ed. G. J. Persley and M. M. Lantin (Washington, D.C.: Consultative Group on International Agricultural Research, 2000).

7. Press conference, London, February 1999, reported in *New Scientist*, February 20, 1999, 4.

8. The Royal Society, "Review of Data on Possible Toxicity of GM Potatoes," in *Promoting Excellence in Science*, at <www.royalsoc.ac.uk>, accessed May 8, 1999.

9. Stanley Ewen and Arpad Pusztai, *Lancet* 354, no. 9187 (October 16, 1999).

10. News, *New Scientist*, October 16, 1999; Emma Ross, "Disputed Study" (Associated Press, October 15, 1999).

11. Lars From, "Gén-roer Gavner Miljøet [GM turnips benefit the environment]," *Jyllands Posten* (Denmark), December 6, 1999.

12. "GMOs Seen as Asia's Saviour, Not Frankenstein Food" (Reuters News Service, November 23, 1999).

13. "Gene-Altered Corn's Impact Reassessed," *Washington Post*, November 3, 1999; Tina Hesman, "Under Milkweed, Monarchs May Sway Fate of High-Tech Crops," *St. Louis Post-Dispatch*, August 7, 2000; Martina McGloughlin, "Biotech Crops: Rely on the Science," *Washington Post*, June 14, 2000, A39; Dan Ferber, "GM Crops in the Cross Hairs," *Science* 286, no. 26 (1999): 1662-66; Carol Haesuk Yoon, "Altered Corn May Imperil Butterfly, Researchers Say," *New York Times*, May 20, 1999, A1; J. Losey, L. Raymor, and M. Carter, "Transgenic Pollen Harms Monarch Larvae," *Nature*, 399 (May 20, 1999): 214.

14. Clive James, "Transgenic Crops Worldwide: Current Situation and Future Outlook" (paper presented at the conference Agricultural Biotechnology in Developing Countries: Toward Optimizing the Benefits for the Poor, Center for Development Research [ZEF], Bonn, November 15–16, 1999).

15. CIMMYT, "Genetic Variations among Major Bread Wheats in the Developing World," in *CIMMYT World Wheat Facts and Trends, 1995/96* (Mexico City: CIMMYT, 1996).

16. "Vaccination Med Frugt [Vaccination with fruit]," *Politiken* (Denmark), March 12, 2000.

Chapter 3. What Is Wrong with More of the Same?

1. Henrik Pontoppidan, "Et Grundskud [A deathblow]," in the short story collection *Fra Hytterne* (Copenhagen, 1887).

2. Per Pinstrup-Andersen, Rajul Pandya-Lorch, and Mark W. Rosegrant, *The World Food Situation: Critical Issues for the Early Twenty-first Century* (Washington, D.C.: IFPRI, 1999).

3. Ibid.

4. Ibid.

5. Serageldin, lecture, Royal Veterinary and Agricultural University.

6. Kim Fleischer Michaelsen, "Nourishment and Undernourishment," in *Good News from Africa*, by Ebbe Schiøler (Washington, D.C.: IFPRI, 1998).

7. Timothy G. Reeves, "Role of International Agricultural Research," in *Biotechnology and Biosafety*, ed. Ismail Serageldin and Wanda Collins (Washington, D.C.: World Bank, 1999).

8. IFPRI, "International Model for Policy Analysis of Commodities and Trade (IMPACT)" (Washington, D.C.: IFPRI, 1999), computer software.

9. Estimated figure, based on the assumption that the reduction in child malnutrition will correspond proportionally to the reduction in the number of hungry people.

10. Figures here and in the remainder of the chapter are from Pinstrup-Andersen, Pandya-Lorch, and Rosegrant, *World Food Situation*.

Chapter 4. The Alternatives

1. Kolstrup, "Kan Generne Trækkes Tilbage?"

2. Møller, "Genteknologiens Betydning."

3. Anthony Trewavas, "Much Food, Many Problems," *Nature* 402 (November 1999): 232.

4. Møller, "Genteknologiens Betydning."

5. Miguel A. Altieri, Peter Rosset, and Lori Ann Thrupp, *The Potential of Agroecology to Combat Hunger in the Developing World*, 2020 Vision Brief no. 55 (Washington, D.C.: IFPRI, 1998).

6. Schiøler, *Good News from Africa.*

7. Norman Borlaug, "Verdens Brød [The world's bread]," *Politiken* (Denmark), November 27, 1999.

8. Schiøler, *Good News from Africa.*

9. Robert L. Paarlberg, *Sustainable Farming: A Political Geography*, 2020 Vision Brief no. 4 (Washington, D.C.: IFPRI, 1994).

10. Borlaug, "Verdens Brød."

11. Ibid.

12. Serageldin and Collins, *Biotechnology and Biosafety*, 157.

13. "Vand-og Sanitetsprogram Bangladesh [Water and hygiene program, Bangladesh]," in *Evaluering 1999/2*, ed. Ismail Serageldin and Wanda Collins (Copenhagen: Royal Danish Ministry of Foreign Affairs, Danida, 1999).

14. Nuffield Council on Bioethics, *Genetically Modified Crops.*

15. Serageldin and Collins, *Biotechnology and Biosafety.*

Chapter 5. Can the Poor Benefit from Genetically Modified Foods?

1. See, for example, Kolstrup, "Kan Generne Trækkes Tilbage?"; and Bo Normander, NOAH, interview on Danish public broadcasting (DR 1) program *Orientering*, March 7, 2000.

2. "Declaration from Physicians and Scientists for Responsible Application of Science and Technology," at <www.psrast.org/dcl>.

3. See, for example, Johan Keller, "Rent Nul! [Zero!]," *Information* (Denmark), January 8-9, 2000.

4. James, "Transgenic Crops Worldwide."

5. Serageldin and Collins, *Biotechnology and Biosafety*, 157.

6. See, for example, Peter Ulvskov's comments in Lykke Thostrup, "Genteknologi Som Ulandsbistand [Genetic technology as development assistance]," in *BioInfo NYT* (Copenhagen: Royal Veterinary and Agricultural University, November 1999); and Per Pinstrup-Andersen, *Modern Biotechnology and Small Farmers in Developing Countries: Commentary* (Washington, D.C.: IFPRI, 1999).

7. See, for example, "Terminator Terminated?" *RAFI News*, at <www.rafi.org>, accessed October 4, 1999; and Hans Herren, discussion at the International Conference on Biotechnology in the Global Econ-

omy, Winnipeg, Canada, September 2-3, 1999, quoted in *Sustainable Developments* 30 (September 6, 1999).

8. Walter Dannigkeit, "Biotechnology from a Global Food Security Perspective" (paper presented at the conference Agricultural Biotechnology in Developing Countries).

9. G. M. Kishore and C. Shewmaker, "Biotechnology: Enhancing Human Nutrition in Developing and Developed Worlds" (paper presented at the colloquium Plants and Population: Is There Time? Irvine, Calif., December 5-6, 1998), here quoted from *Proceedings of the National Academy of Sciences* [online] 96 (May 25, 1999), at <www.pnas.org/cgi/content>.

10. Vernon W. Ruttan, "Biotechnology and Agriculture: A Skeptical Perspective," *AgBio Forum* 2 (winter 1999), at <www.agbioforum.missouri.ed/agbioforum>.

11. Henk Hobbelink, "Nyt Håb Eller Falske Løfter? Bioteknologien og Den Tredje Verdens Landbrug [New hope or false promises? Biotechnology and third world agriculture]" (Copenhagen: NOAH, 1988).

12. M. Morris and D. Hoisington, "Bringing the Benefits of Biotechnology to the Poor: The Role of the CGIAR Centers" (paper presented at the conference Agricultural Biotechnology in Developing Countries).

13. M. Hossain et al., "Biotechnology Research in Rice for Asia: Priorities, Focus and Directions" (paper presented at the conference Agricultural Biotechnology in Developing Countries).

14. Ibid.

15. W. B. Frommer et al., "Taking Transgenic Plants with a Pinch of Salt," *Science* 285 (August 20, 1999).

16. "Iron-fortified Rice" (Nature Biotechnology Press Release, Nature, March 1999).

17. D. T. Avery, "Golden Rice Could Combat Third World Malnutrition," *Bridge News Forum,* August 27, 1999.

18. F. Wambugu, "Why Africa Needs Agricultural Biotech," *Nature* 400 (July 1, 1999).

19. "Boosting Insect Biocontrol" (Nature Press Release, Nature, November 1999).

20. Karby Leggett and Ian Johnson, *China Bets Farm on Promise of Genetic Engineering* (New York: Dow Jones/Wall Street Journal, March 29, 2000).

21. M. Qaim, *The Economic Effects of Genetically Modified Orphan Commodities: Projections for Sweetpotato in Kenya* (Bonn: ISAAA and Center for Development Research [ZEF], 1999).

22. M. Qaim, "Potential Benefits of Agricultural Biotechnology: An Example from the Mexican Potato Sector," *Review of Agricultural Economics* 21, no. 2 (2000).

Chapter 6. Who Sets the Agenda?

1. Adamu, "We'll Feed Our People as We See Fit."

2. Jennifer A. Thomson, "Developing Country's Can't Wait and See," at <www.cid.harvard.edu/cidbiotech/comments/comments69.htm>, accessed July 28, 2000.

3. African Biotechnology Stakeholders' Forum, "RE: Biotechnology and Kenya's Socioeconomic Survival" (Nairobi, Kenya, September 1999).

4. P. Chengal Reddy, "When Western Activism Is Misguided," personal communication, 2000.

5. <www.greenpeace.dk/www/kampagner/gen2.html>.

6. Niels Nørgaard, "Jagt På Gensplejset Mad [Hunt for GM food]," *Politiken* (Denmark), January 9, 2000.

7. "Sund Gris Bliver Dyr [Healthy pigs could prove costly]," *Politiken* (Denmark), January 15, 2000.

8. *Independent* (London), January 15, 2001.

9. *Wall Street Journal*, February 21, 2001.

10. Per Pinstrup-Andersen, "Den Globale Fødevareforsyning [The global food supply]" (paper presented at Landsplanteavlsmøde i Århus, Denmark, January 19, 2000).

11. Ibid.

12. Niels Nørgaard, "Klar Besked om Gener [A clear message on genes]," *Politiken* (Denmark), January 9, 2000.

13. "French Pet Food Co Goes GM (genetically modified)-free," *Agrow* 20, September 1999; personal communication from staff member, World Bank.

14. "Greenpeace til Auken: EU Må Tage Gen-skepsis Alvorligt [Greenpeace to Auken: E.U. must take GM-skepticism seriously]" (Greenpeace Denmark press release, December 10, 1999).

15. Frank J. Mitsch and Jenifer S. Mitchell, "DuPont, Ag Biotech: Thanks, But No Thanks" (New York: Deutsche Bank, July 12, 1999).

16. Merete Nielsen, "Ingen Vil Hjælpe Monsanto [Nobody will help Monsanto]," *Information* (Denmark), January 13, 2000.

17. Rick Weiss, "EPA Restricts Gene-Altered Corn in Response to Concerns: Farmers Must Plant Conventional 'Refuges' to Reduce Threat of

Ecological Damage," *Washington Post*, January 16, 2000.

18. Dennis T. Avery, "Environmentalists Are Hunting the Biotech Foods Revolution, but Corporate Missteps and Farmers Are Giving Them Plenty of Help," *Bridge News Forum*, January 7, 2000; Mitsch and Mitchell, "DuPont, Ag Biotech."

19. "USA Vil Begrænse Brug af Génmajs [The United States will constrain the case of GM maize]," *Information* (Denmark), January 17, 2000; "Brazil Farmers Smuggle, Plant GM Soy," *AgBiotech Reporter*, October 1999.

20. "Seeds of Trouble," *Wall Street Journal*, September 15, 1999.

21. John Tavis, "Vatican Experts OK Plant, Animal Genetic Engineering," *St. Louis Review*, October 22, 1999.

22. "The Church of England Statement on Genetically Modified Organisms" (London: Church of England, April 1999).

23. Jonathan Petre, "Church Bans GM Crop Trials on Its Land," *Sunday Telegraph*, December 5, 1999.

24. "When Did Rice Become Corn?"

25. Nuffield Council on Bioethics, "Genetically Modified Crops

Chapter 7. Moving Forward

1. Morton Satin, *Food Irradiation: A Guidebook*, 2d ed. (Lancaster, Penn.: Technomic Publishing, 1996).

2. Michael Palmgren, Royal Veterinary and Agricultural University, lecture on Agenda 2000, Allerslev, Denmark, February 17, 2000.

3. Gordon Conway, "The Rockefeller Foundation and Plant Biotechnology" (address to Monsanto management, June 1999).

4. Gordon Conway, "Crop Biotechnology: Benefits, Risks, and Ownership" (paper presented at the biotechnology conference sponsored by the Organization for Economic Cooperation and Development, Edinburgh, February 28–March 1, 2000).

5. "'Terminator' Seed Sterility Technology Dropped" (Rockefeller Foundation news advisory, October 4, 1999), at <www.rockfound.org>.

6. <www.christian-aid.org.uk>, accessed February 2000.

7. Bo Normander, "Husk de Bæredygtige Løsninger [Remember the sustainable solutions]," *Politiken* (Denmark), March 5, 2000.

8. Telephone conversations with several Danish NGOs: IBIS, Folkekirkens Nødhjælp, and Mellemfolkeligt Samvirke, March 2000.

9. Brian D. Wright, "IPR Challenges and International Research Col-

laborations in Agricultural Biotechnology" (paper presented at the conference Agricultural Biotechnology in Developing Countries).

10. Jeffrey Sachs, "Helping the World's Poorest," *Economist*, August 14, 1999.

11. Lykke Thostrup, "Roer for Sig og Raps for Sig [Turnips on their own, rape on its own]," in *BioInfo NYT*.

INDEX

Page numbers in *italics* indicate material presented in boxes.

search priorities for, 92, 97–100;
research programs established
for, 12–13; and right to refuse
GM products, 108, 133–34; seed
saving in, 136; silent hunger in,
59–60; yield gap in, 28, 30
Diagnostics, 36
Disasters: in developing world,
58–59, 70–71
Distribution of food supply, 5–6,
69–70, 73–75
Doubly Green Revolution, 20
DuPont, 117, 118

East Asia: potential for increased
agricultural production in, 68
Eating habits: predictions about,
65–66
Environment: and better crop
yields, 67; genetically modified
food and, 43–44, 51, 95, 133;
Green Revolution and, 19–20;
irrigation and, 81–82; organic
farming and, 75–76
Environmental organizations: response to GM foods, 109–10,
114–15
Ethical issues: of genetic engineering, 118–23
Ethiopia: cattle in, 78
Europe: response to GM foods,
112–15
European Union: response to GM
foods, 113–14; safety standards
of, 40–41

Famine, threat of: in developing
world, 10–11, 13, 30. *See also*
Starvation
FAO. *See* Food and Agriculture Organization

Farmland: poor condition of, 54,
68–69
Feed grains: genetically modified,
from developing countries, 94
Fertilizer(s): lack of, in Africa, 28,
78–79; organic viewpoint on,
78–79; and productivity, 82; re-
duced need for, 52, 54
Food and Agriculture Organiza-
tion (FAO), 63
Food consumption: trends in,
65–66
Food enrichment. *See* Nutrition
Food production. *See* Production
Food supply: distribution of (*see*
Distribution of food supply); fu-
ture of, 62–64, 81–83
Ford Foundation, 12
Foreign aid: decrease in, 30–31;
and prevention of starvation, 11;
projected demand for, 69–70;
state of, 73
Frankenfood, 109
Free trade: and GM food regula-
tions, 133
Functional genes, 33

Gene banks, 28, 29
Gene dispersal: by GM plants, fear
of, 49–50, 133
Gene gun, 39
Gene manipulation. *See* Genetic
engineering
Gene mapping, 35, 36, 37
Genes, 33; shutting off, 93; species
and, 32, 33–34, 121–22
Gene splicing, 36, 38–39; precision
of, 40
Genetically modified food: ad-
vances in, 50–56, 93–95; case-by-
case approach to, 143–45; criti-